KW-554-810

Record keeping in the progressive primary school

635010

WALLINGTON

This book is to be returned on or before
the last date stamped below.

STORE
14 MAR 78

MC 18.3.72
20. APR. 1972
To Sutton 6/6/72
-1. NOV. 1972
29 November
29. 03. 73
28. 04. 73
04. 06. 73
27. 09. 73
14. 11. 73
08. 02. 74

09. 03. 74
06. 04. 74
Ren 3.9.74
27. 11. 74
13. MAY 7
03. OCT 75
12. MAY 76
18. SEP 76

27 DEC 1992
LASER
- 8 JUL 1988
+ 2 months

LONDON BOROUGH OF SUTTON
WALLINGTON LIBRARY
SHOTFIELD, WALLINGTON
01-647 4458/9

30119 019 422 908
London Borough of Sutton

Record keeping in the progressive primary school

Peter Rance

Ward Lock Educational

ISBN 0 7062 3318 2

©Peter Rance 1971. All rights reserved. No part of this publication may be reproduced, stored in a retrieval system, or transmitted, in any form or by any means, electronic, mechanical, photocopying, recording or otherwise, without the prior permission of the copyright owner.

First published 1971

WAL
LONDON BOROUGH
OF SUTTON
PUBLIC LIBRARIES
635010
10 SEP 1971
371.2

Set in 11 on 12 point Monotype Baskerville
by Neill and Co Ltd, Edinburgh
for Ward Lock Educational Limited
116 Baker Street, London WIM 2BB
Printed in Great Britain

Contents

Introduction 9

Part one **The background to record keeping**

General background 13
Why keep teaching records? 14
What should a good record be like? 15
What a record should not do 16
Record keeping problems 16
What other details should be recorded? 17
Other kinds of records 18
Team teaching and record keeping 19
A child's record of his work 19
Records and the school secretary 19
General conclusion 20

Part two **Various methods of record keeping**

General comment 25
Indexed or 'date ordered' record books 25
Histograms and graphs 25
Pie diagrams 26
Multiple choice or 'cross out' records 26
Data cards 27
Photographic records 27
Filmstrips 27
Cine camera and tape recordings 27
Miniature tape recorders 27
Colour slides 28
Video tape 28
Cumulative records 28
Other recording and planning procedures 28
Conclusion 28

Part three Illustrated examples of various records

A parent's pre-school profile 33
A personality record: one 36
two 38
Educational reports for parents 40
The data card system 42
A teacher's record of the integrated day 46
A child's record of the integrated day 49
Recording a class activity 51
A reading progress record: one 53
two 56
A reading workshop record sheet 58
An infant school mathematics record 60
Recording assignment cards used in infant mathematics schemes 63
Mathematics record: one 66
two 69
A discovery or activity record sheet 72
Recording achievement on standardized tests 74
A graph of attainment scores 77
Recording the academic attainment level of a school 78
Recording the results of NFER tests 80
Recording swimming attainment 82
A headteacher's report to the school governors 84
Three dimensional record keeping 88
Bibliography 91
Index 93

Introduction

As our primary schools sweep along on the incoming tide of new teaching techniques, many teachers find that the old methods they have used to record the various facets of their work are becoming increasingly inadequate. There is a real need for some method of recording the progress of children who are working in an informal situation, although unfortunately it is difficult to devise one which is not only efficient but will also remain intelligible at a later date.

This book has been written against the constantly changing background of new teaching methods and my own experience of the difficulties involved with such work. The suggestions it contains are mainly based on those forms of record keeping which have been successfully used under these circumstances and are offered as a foundation upon which each school can build a system of record keeping which will meet its own requirements.

P.B.R. 1970

PART ONE
The background to record keeping

The background to record keeping

General background

One result of the present trend towards a more informal approach to children's educational needs is the breakdown of subject barriers in the primary school curriculum. As the traditional barriers disappear the subjects merge together so that the children's interest in learning can be actively maintained over a longer period of time. Similarly our method of organizing a classroom has evolved to the point where it is no longer necessary for every child in a class or age group to study exactly the same problem at exactly the same time. 'Family grouping' and the 'integrated day' encourage children to spend considerable lengths of time exploring the various aspects of a particular subject which interests them, and teachers have been persuaded that it is perhaps wiser to consider a period of a week or more as a reasonable length of time in which a child can achieve a balanced timetable which covers a variety of subjects.

The problem of how to record what is actually taking place within a class under these conditions faces all teachers who adopt less formal methods of organization. The purpose of this book is to highlight the difficulties encountered and suggest some possible answers.

Some local education authorities, such as Stoke on Trent, have already made determined efforts to coordinate and standardize the record of a child's progress through their schools. Unfortunately the individual requirements of both schools and children will differ from area to area and the whole approach to record keeping in this country is very casual. Admittedly too efficient and systematic a recording of a child's school life can prove self defeating, especially when based entirely upon written or verbal attainment tests, for these can be disastrous for the growth of the primary school child if they are subsequently used as a basis for streaming at the secondary level. Happily most teachers are conscious of the danger of hanging a particular label on a child as it is recognized that children tend to actively reflect such labels.

As a result of the dangers inherent in such testing some schools are trying to develop an alternative systematic method of recording a child's achievements, interests, aspirations and personal qualities. In fact when the problem is viewed overall a cumulative type of record seems the most sensible. It should start with the pre-school background provided by the parents and follow a child's progress through the various educational establishments attended, so that it can form a firm basis for any far reaching decisions which have to be taken. Within this record many different types of records will be kept as the child develops and this should help counter any temporary misfortune the child may encounter during his educational career.

This kind of individual progress dossier should not be our only concern, for with the gradual development of education itself there is also a need to record how a child is being taught.

Why keep teaching records?

Some people may argue that any detailed record of a new system of teaching rapidly makes it become inflexible and once flexibility is lost, no fresh discoveries will be made. If this is true it may well be asked how teachers are supposed to find out that a new discovery has been made if no records of their past activities are available.

Similarly among the welter of new teaching methods now in vogue there is a tendency to assume, without a great deal of proof, that they are better than those which preceeded them. Indeed we may soon be in danger of worrying too much about how our schools are organized and not enough about the depth and quality of understanding our pupils acquire. How can it be proved that the informal approach to education is successful if only inadequate records are kept? How, over a period of years, can there be a realistic assessment of the effective and ineffective aspects of this approach? How can it be shown that such methods can enable every child to build up a balanced view of life as a result of a well balanced contact with the many aspects of human knowledge? Surely the only answer to these questions is to maintain a suitable record of teaching methods, school organization, and the progress of each child. If schools do not keep meaningful records from which reliable conclusions can be drawn, they may well find themselves bogged down in an educational morass of their own making.

To sum up we must conclude that record keeping is important for the following reasons:

1 To assess what has been achieved in the past, and to show the rate of progress at present and the direction in which the overall development of a school's education is moving.

2 To record the method of organization and the type of work being undertaken. Teachers will be able to learn from hind sight provided they have well documented facts to look at.

3 To record the progress of individual children and their attainment in specific subjects so that their future education can be suitably planned. This does not mean that every moment of every activity has to be recorded, but there will be times when a detailed record of a specific subject, such as attainment in reading, will be of great assistance in teaching the child.

4 To be able to compare the academic attainment of one child with another which can be useful, especially where large families are concerned. Team teaching also requires a record of a child's academic progress when behaviour and work problems arise.
5 To study a child's progress record in order to discover academic flaws requiring remedial treatment, e.g. to help identify backward readers in the lower school.
6 To record the rate of progress in a child's physical and social development. Very often the *rate* of progress in such matters is more important than the actual level of attainment achieved.
7 To facilitate the movement of children from one school to another. Our society is becoming increasingly mobile so it is important that the movement of children from primary to primary, and primary to secondary school is made as smooth as possible.
8 To promote greater cooperation between schools by enabling detailed discussions of mutual problems to take place. Teachers must be able to quote specific examples if such problems are to be solved. This can only be done if well kept records are available.

What should a good record be like?

Records play an important part in all walks of life. Some are large, visually attractive but pointless, while others, like our bank statements, are meagre and meaningful. Bearing this in mind the following points may be regarded as the basic elements of any records which are devised:

1 They must be easy to keep. Only the barest minimum of a teacher's time should be devoted to maintaining them. Above all they must fulfil a specific task and still be informative when reconsidered years later.
2 They should be simple to understand and based on knowledge which is common to all teachers. A well kept record based on some obscure system is of no help when a child transfers from one school to another.
3 A record should be constructive, i.e. it should provide enough detail about a subject for a balanced judgment to be made by another teacher.
4 If possible a record should be versatile since any record which serves two functions saves time. For example a child's progress record can be made by storing the school reports sent home to his parents (see page 41).
5 All records should enable additional facts to be constructed from them which will reveal any general trends in a child's or a school's progress.
6 Any overall record should provide some means whereby quick reference can be made to the more detailed information from which its general conclusions were drawn. Thus any record of a school's academic progress should be based upon the records of individual children (see graph on page 79).
7 All records kept by children concerning their own development should be designed to show only a growth of achievement. In this way a child

will be encouraged to further effort by his past successes, e.g. the simple display graph of a child's progress in learning to swim on page 83.

As each stage is reached so a child's confidence in his ability to swim will grow and the graph will indicate to both teacher and child which task has to be tackled next.

What a record should not do

A young teacher once said, 'I can make a record of what I hope to achieve each week but how do I know I've achieved what I set out to do?'

With informal methods of teaching a teacher may have a general concept rather than a precise idea of what she is setting out to achieve during the course of a particular day's teaching. In these circumstances it must be accepted that there is a distinct difference between forecasting intentions and recording what has been achieved, but unfortunately this extremely important point is not understood by some people and they treat forecasts as if they were records. However, the following points ignore the question of *forecasting* or *pre-planning* and concern themselves with recording only.

1 Records should never waste a teacher's time, especially when that time could be used to prepare for a teaching session.
2 Records should never be used to check that a teacher has undertaken a certain piece of work. There are better ways for a headmaster to solve this problem.
3 Records should not be written in educational jargon or so detailed that the basic facts become obscured.
4 A record should never be kept unless it will be relevant at a later stage in a child's career. For example does it really matter when young Tom reached the top of the climbing frame for the first time? Surely the fact that he has failed to do so by the age of ten is far more important. In other words, if something is normal why bother to record it?
5 Only a record which has a specific purpose is worth keeping.

This last rule promotes two possible lines of thought: teachers must either make a point of recording only the unusual, or decide to record only those essential details which will be required at a particular time in the future, for example when transferring to another school or when additional evidence of academic attainment is required for CSE.

Record keeping problems

It has already been suggested that school records must be simple, easy to keep, constructive and cross indexed, but without doubt their most important characteristic is that they should always fulfil a specific function at a later date. An extremely detailed record of each child's daily progress will become progressively self defeating because analysis of such a rapidly expanding mass of verbage will be a formidable task. Similarly a teacher with thirty children in her charge will produce such a large document in such a short time that any assessment of newly introduced teaching techniques will prove a time consuming task. If such a teacher is also asked to record the activities of her class as a whole the problem immediately doubles in complexity.

Another problem which arises is the question of what period of time a record should be designed to cover. Here it is always wise to remember that children take many years to grow and changes in their personality and academic attainment normally take place fairly slowly. On the other hand if there is a drastic and permanent change in some direction there must be a means of recording what has taken place. Happily such changes do not happen more than once or twice even with the most unusual child, so the problem of recording them is relatively small.

From this short synopsis of the difficulties facing a teacher responsible for thirty or more young children it can be seen that the best method of assessing overall progress is to record it only at evenly spaced intervals of time. If teachers are content to record only those aspects of a child which are unusual, then a time span of six months or a year is quite reasonable. If there is also some system for alternating or rotating the method of assessment, a clearer picture of each child will be obtained.

In this way a system of record keeping can be developed on the principle that the majority of the children will progress quite normally and that there is little need for more than a termly assessment of their personalities. This is particularly true when a teacher has continuous personal contact with each child.

Success with this system can be achieved by completing a personality record each November and March and taking a series of standardized attainment tests in May each year. As can be seen on page 76, the annual use of a standardized test can, if plotted on a graph, illustrate a child's rate of attainment over a period of years. Such statistics can also be used to assess the academic standard of a school if they are displayed as shown on page 79.

Teachers will also discover that there is a real need to record the progress a child makes in grasping certain basic skills, such as learning to read. However the basic principles of recording as previously outlined still apply to this task and various systems are shown on pages 53 to 59.

What other details should be recorded?

Having agreed that some record of a child's rate of learning is necessary, it has also been suggested that there is no need to comment on every small detail. Teachers should apply exactly the same principle to the following records.

Health and physical development

Any absence of more than three weeks should be recorded with the dates and reason. Teachers should also be encouraged to pass comment upon a child's general health, if necessary, as such observations can sometimes reveal a serious medical problem. Lack of attainment rather than attainment in the child's physical development should be noted.

Personality

A half page comment by the child's teacher each November and March can reveal the main features of a child's character when combined with similar comments from other teachers over a period of years (see page 37 for example). Alternatively the data card on page 45 or the school report on page 41 can be used for this purpose.

Academic attainment

If any record is required other than those already mentioned, it should be sufficient to record the best and the worst features only. The key point is to record what a child understands rather than what he does. Similarly the rate at which a child makes progress is frequently more important than the actual academic level he has reached.

Social background, emotional and psychological problems

This kind of confidential record must be kept by a headteacher, or head of department. The need for such a record will only arise when the personality record outlined previously does not meet the needs of either the teacher or the child. (See page 39 for the outline of a personality record which could be the basis for requesting a psychiatric or medical report.)

Other kinds of records

So far it is the child who has dominated our thoughts about record keeping and the role of the headteacher has only been hinted at. There are some aspects of a school however which fall entirely within the scope of his responsibility. It is the headteacher's task to assess the success or failure of each newly devised teaching technique, apparatus or scheme of work which is introduced into the school. Similarly he should know how every child is progressing under the care of each member of staff and whether the children are obtaining a well balanced education. Where a headteacher is likely to remain in a school for a number of years it will be useful for him to have a record of how the school has developed under his care. This can easily be achieved if he submits a written report to the school governors prior to each of their termly meetings. (See pages 85 to 87 for an example of its contents.)

It is also accepted that a headteacher is ultimately responsible for the progressive development of each child in the school and he must therefore devise some system for quickly refreshing his memory when faced with the parents of any particular child.

Unfortunately it is at this particular point that many classteachers' record keeping problems begin, for some headteachers rely too heavily on records for such details and this in turn leads to teachers being expected to keep over elaborate records about children. This system also has a habit of breaking down under stress for nothing can replace a personal knowledge of the child concerned and such knowledge can only be gained through personal contact with every child in the school over the course of a week or ten days. On the other hand an easily assimilated synopsis of a child's personality is of considerable help when parents arrive unexpectedly.

It is also the duty of the headteacher to establish an administrative structure within a school which will enable all returns and records demanded by the Minister of Education or the local education authority to be completed accurately. This is no light task and where copies of such records can help build up a useful record of the school's development, they should be used for this purpose.

Team teaching and record keeping

In a team teaching situation keeping records will become more complicated. Each record will have to serve the requirements of a number of teachers; one teacher's entry may require suitable follow up work to be undertaken by another member of the same teaching team; it is also likely that a child will respond to each member of the team in a different way. In addition to these problems the various aspects of a child's progress will be recorded by different teachers and this will mean that a child's record must always be kept up to date if the most suitable type of work is to be prepared for the child.

Under these conditions a specific period of time each week must be allocated to record keeping and an efficient method of storage devised. The teaching team should assemble in one place to complete individual record cards so that any problems which arise can be discussed informally before any written entry is made on a child's record card. Of course not every child will need to be discussed in this manner for the procedure will only apply in those cases where a joint approach by all members of the team is required. If a special room can be allocated for these record keeping activities, so much the better.

A child's record of his work

Photographs of wall displays, class folders, graphs and models can all prove excellent ways of recording a class's educational progress. For individual work such as mathematics, a child can maintain a record of his progress on a sheet of paper similar to those shown on pages 70 and 71.

Children may also record their progress by keeping for future reference any individual booklet or classwork which has been compiled as a result of their joint activities. For a comprehensive survey of this subject read *Teaching by Topics* (Ward Lock Educational, 1969).

Storing such classwork may prove to be very difficult in some schools but it is very worthwhile, even if it means a fresh start has to be made each year (where a year's work is photographed storage problems are eliminated) as it is an ideal method of keeping a record. It saves time, clearly indicates the type of teaching employed and the standard reached by a class or group. If the children are encouraged to put their name and age on any piece of work they produce it will be far more revealing than a few hurriedly written notes in a teacher's record book.

Records and the school secretary

The ever increasing burden of school administration coupled with the need for a school to create a good public image has resulted in the post of school secretary becoming more important. Indeed all new school buildings recognize this fact by providing office accommodation for the secretary where she can take over various tasks which will help lighten the burden of record keeping that normally falls on the teaching staff.

One of the ways in which she can help is by maintaining an accurate list of children in each class, in chronological order, giving each child's exact age as on September 1st each year. Another list of children with the telephone number at which their parents can be contacted during the working day or the address of a near relative is of great value on many occasions.

The secretary who types details for sports day, educational visits, camps, visitors days, PTA etc can make herself very popular if she takes care to file a copy of such items for future reference. This is extremely helpful where staff changes are frequent and teachers find themselves responsible for such activities for the first time.

A well maintained file of the headteacher's reports to the school governors can prove an invaluable record to a headteacher over a number of years. This record can also be an ideal way of enabling a new headteacher to grasp the substance of any long standing problem associated with the school. (See pages 85 to 87 for a possible layout.)

General conclusion

There are three golden rules for record keeping:

1 Keep as few records as possible.
2 Be constantly on the lookout for some method of reducing those already in existence.
3 Regularly revise those that are in constant use.

PART TWO
Various methods of record keeping

Various methods of record keeping

General comment

With the pressing need to record so many aspects of a large number of children over a period of five or six years, almost all educational records must contain a large element of visual display if they are to be easily understood and this is illustrated by the type of record shown on page 79. Until suitable computers are made available to schools for this task, teachers are considerably restricted in their choice of presentation because the number of methods which allow visual representation is limited.

This problem has become even more noticeable with the introduction of informal teaching methods. In fact with this type of school environment the old style Teacher's Record Book with its neatly ruled pages for Test Results does not meet the new recording demands of informal teaching and is completely inadequate.

Indexed or 'date ordered' record books

The commonly used Teacher's Record Book was reasonably suitable for the simple task of recording teacher directed work undertaken by a class over a period of one week. It was never suitable for assessing what had been understood by the children in that class over the period of a week, a month, a term, or a year.

With so many schools still clinging to this method of recording it is difficult to see what will happen when they start using informal, integrated methods of teaching. How will teachers be able to record all the diverse activities simultaneously taking place in the classroom? In these circumstances it might be possible to record the activities of each child in an individual record book, but who would seriously suggest that a teacher should walk around with thirty thin record books just to record each child's activities?

We can summarize this problem by agreeing that the old type of record book may be useful if there is a real need to record the activities of a small group of children. However, it is rather difficult to see the point of such an exercise unless it forms part of a larger research project which starts out to discover specific facts concerning group working.

Histograms and graphs

Both histograms and graphs are among the most popular methods of recording or displaying all types of information. They are simple, effective and easily understood. A more complex type of graph is illustrated on page 76.

Where standardized attainment tests are employed, the results can be displayed by means of various graphs which will reveal the general trends of a child's progress through the school.

A three dimensional histogram can be constructed on transparent material. This technique is made more effective if black is used to colour the first histogram and each subsequent histogram is drawn up in a progressively lighter colour. When these sheets are placed on top of each other the histogram reveals the progressive development of each piece of information it contains.

Pie diagrams

A pie diagram can be used when the total sum of information that has to be recorded is known in advance. To do this with many informal methods is almost impossible, but pie diagrams can be used in an informal teaching situation to ensure that each child spends a minimum amount of time on each subject, for they swiftly reveal where a child is taking an unbalanced approach to his work.

One problem with this type of record is that it will take a part of a teacher's time each day if it is to be effective. Another difficulty which must be recognized is that if it is to be useful, a pie diagram must be neat and accurate. An example is shown on page 47.

Multiple choice or 'cross out' records

This can be a good system of record keeping provided it is constructed in such a way that it does not become a rigid work syllabus which the teacher is expected to follow slavishly. To be successful the record should provide for the possibility of carrying out the work involved in a number of different ways. This can usually be accomplished if the record contains a number of alternative subjects at each level of attainment or provides for the work to be undertaken in a number of different sequences. (For examples of this kind of record see pages 57 and 67.)

This type of record is constructed by listing all the stages of development in a subject in a logically progressive sequence and then arranging some method for showing when a child reaches each stage. Adequate space must be provided for any comment a teacher wishes to make and the date when each development occurred. The basic structure of this type of record must be revised at least once a year to ensure that it keeps pace with any new teaching techniques, new textbooks and new apparatus.

Having pointed out its chief characteristics it can be seen that basically the 'cross out' record can be used wherever stages of learning are reasonably predictable. Obviously learning to read and understanding basic mathematical concepts will fall into this category.

Experience shows that this kind of record is easy to keep and quickly provides essential information about a child. With thirty or forty children in a class the whole record is quite manageable provided that only the basic tools of learning are recorded. In fact up to the age of eleven there is little point in keeping a record of any other academic subjects.

This method of recording can be abused just as easily as any other. If it is to be really useful the teacher must include a short comment on the child's progress when difficulties are experienced.

Data cards

These cards (approximately 100 mm × 100 mm) are punched with a series of holes to allow a swift collation of a limited number of known facts about a class of children. Data cards are very useful in large schools where information on the various types of children in the school is required at short notice.

Once a card is correctly named and dated it is completed by opening up the holes on the card which do not apply to the child concerned. Any relevant information about a child is indicated by a complete hole. For further details see pages 43 to 45.

Photographic records

Most teachers have met the kind of school photographer who supplies a school with a free miniature copy of the coloured photograph he hopes to sell to each child's parents. In large schools attaching these photos to the record cards of the children can prove very helpful.

Other photographers, such as the Scholastic Souvenir Company of Blackpool, also provide a service whereby they photograph any school work or activity and subsequently provide either large scale photos or a coloured filmstrip complete with subtitles.

Filmstrips

A versatile method of recording various school activities over a period of time is a forty frame filmstrip. It is cheap, effective and can be easily stored for quick reference at any future date.

Cine camera and tape recordings

Obviously a cine camera and a sound tape recorder are ideal methods of recording school activities which are considered worth keeping for future generations of children to see and hear. Where such recording is done on a systematic basis it can provide a vivid way of assessing the development of teaching techniques in a school over many years.

Miniature tape recorders

Any teacher who has had the patience to use a cassette tape recorder on an educational visit will know the value of such a record during follow up work in the classroom. The sound of a train, a giggle, a snatch of bird song, when replayed in the classroom can rekindle the atmosphere of a visit, brighten up a a damp day and provide an entire class of children with new ideas and impressions many weeks after the visit has taken place.

Colour slides

The Kodac Instamatic cassette loading camera can almost be classified as the poor man's passport to recording classroom activities in colour. If the storage of the resulting colour slides is well organized, fifty slides of a year's work can prove to be a more valuable record than five volumes of the conventional record book.

When used to record the development of topic work within a school this method was found to be both practical and informative. It is also interesting to note that teachers deliberately found time to study up to fifty or more coloured slides of previous topics, to find ideas which might be redeveloped, or to refresh their minds concerning some past success they had experienced with informal work.

Video tape

With the increasing use of closed circuit television in colleges of education and other higher education establishments, it can only be a matter of time before such equipment is available in primary schools. When this happens, video tape will provide an extremely suitable method of recording the individual activities of various groups in a school and the behaviour pattern of any 'problem' children.

Cumulative records

The need for an adequate record of each child's school life which will also facilitate a smooth transfer from one school to another is recognized by most local education authorities who issue a form suitable for this purpose.

These cumulative record cards tend to follow a basic pattern which expects each child to be listed under such subheadings as Child's name, Address, Name of parent or guardian, Date of birth, Position in family, Father's occupation, Emotional and social development, Home environment, Schools attended, Nursery school record, Results of objective and diagnostic tests, Health record, Record of interests and activities, Academic record, Headteachers' remarks. The Scottish Education Department pamphlet, *Pupils Progress Records* (HMSO 1969) provides a well balanced assessment of this particular facet of record keeping.

Other recording and planning procedures

In the third part of this book several examples have been included of records which do not strictly fall under one of the headings given above.

Some of these records can be applied to modern teaching techniques. Others have a special function to perform in helping a staff to see the general development in the educational techniques they employ. To make the reader's task easier a detailed explanation is given opposite each method of recording illustrated.

Conclusion

With the introduction of child centred education into our schools the problem of assessing what information should be retained for future reference and how best to record it nags at the conscience of many teachers trying to increase their understanding of informal teaching methods.

There are some educationists who genuinely believe that all record keeping only wastes valuable time which could be better employed in preparing to teach the children. However some teachers find that by recording their activities they establish a firm base from which to discover fresh techniques and thereby improve their teaching.

When record keeping is considered against this background of diverse educational thought it is most interesting to see how a rough system of classification develops through the constant recurrence of such words as permanent, temporary, continuous, spasmodic, regular, individual, class and school. For example records such as log books and governors' reports which will be kept over many years can be thought of as both continuous and permanent records. Similarly the detailed record of a child's progress in learning to read will be of great importance until the skill is fully mastered. Then a short synopsis can be permanently recorded on the child's individual record or data card. Once this has been done the continuous and detailed record of reading can be destroyed as its status changes to that of a temporary record card.

Similarly attainment and IQ tests may be taken in a school at regular or spasmodic intervals, and the way in which they are recorded will automatically reflect the amount of importance the school attaches to such results. Class or group activities may be permanently recorded on film or displayed as a temporary exhibition.

When the abundance of school, class and individual work which results from informal teaching is coupled with the wide variety of recording methods available it is not surprising that teachers wonder what to keep and what to ignore. Obviously in these conditions haphazard recording is quite useless but a highly organized and rigidly enforced system of record keeping also defeats its own purpose, for by its very nature it tends to introduce the worst features of competition by creating feelings of inadequacy among either the less able pupils or staff. While there appears nothing wrong with reducing records to the barest minimum, over elaboration seems just as undesirable as the complete lack of any system for recording the progress of a child or school.

Obviously the record keeping requirements of every school will, like every teacher and child in each school, be different. The purpose of this book is to provide teachers with an initial basis for thought about the problem and to act as a small reminder to those who are dedicated to recording every small detail that good records must be simple, easily understood and regularly revised.

PART THREE
Illustrated examples of various records

Illustrated examples of various records

A parent's pre-school profile

By the time most children enter an infant school they have already had a number of illnesses and will have certainly developed a character. Most schools however do not request parents to supply these sort of details, perhaps because they are afraid that all parents see their geese as swans although the experience of American schools in this field contradicts this criticism. But surely if a synopsis of a child's pre-school life is made available to teachers they need spend less time assessing a child's background and have a firmer base upon which to start their teaching?

In France every child's pre-school details are provided by his parents and these form the beginning of a dossier which is subsequently added to throughout the child's school life. However pre-school records such as the letter and form on pages 34 and 35 will have to be treated with some caution, although even the fact that a mother's assessment of her child is completely wrong is in itself of great value to a teacher.

General comment

The letter on page 34 can be sent to parents within the first week of a child's school life. If it is possible to include an invitation to a social function at the same time this will provide an excellent opportunity for an informal discussion, with parents, of any problems which arise. A welcoming tea party or coffee morning for new parents run by the well established members of the PTA would be ideal.

To reduce the number of records, the relevant details supplied by the parents should be entered on the official school record card and the pre-school record destroyed.

Fordbury Primary School
Fitch Green
Nr. Hertford

Tel. Hertford 32396

Dear Mr and Mrs ....Hill........

Now that your child has entered this school we look forward to her/him continuing to develop as a pleasant sociable child with many personal talents.

Obviously you will have the most important part to play in this process but complete success can only be achieved where there is constant and close cooperation between a child's home and school.

With this in mind we would ask you to help us to cater for the needs of your child by completing as many details on the reverse of this letter as possible. This information will be treated as confidential but it will greatly assist your child's teacher to adopt the right approach to your child's needs.

Should you prefer to call and talk to me personally I will be delighted to see you, or alternatively you may prefer to speak to me about this matter on the telephone.

All the staff and I hope your child will have a happy and successful school life.

Yours sincerely

J. T. Thomas

Headteacher

Dear Parents,

Please be kind enough to complete as many of the following details as possible.

Your child's full name STEPHEN JOHN HILL

Address or telephone number at which you can be contacted out of school hours. (We already have your home address.)

Hertford 901

Does your child suffer from ill health? ~~yes~~ or no

If you wish you may give brief details..................

....

It will be of great help to us if you will put an X in the small square you consider best describes your child.

	Always	Usually	Sometimes	Seldom	Never
Helps with activities in the home			X		
Plays happily with other children			X		
Shows interest in his surroundings		X			
Keeps himself amused		X			
Speaks clearly	X				
Talks freely to strangers				X	
Good memory for people and places		X			
Can count up to ten objects		X			
Dresses himself	X				
Feeds himself	X				
Goes to the toilet by himself	X				
Puts on his own shoes		X			
Likes paddling in water	X				

Write any other information which you think will be of help to us when teaching your child.

As we live on a farm Stephen has not been used to mixing with a large number of children.

A personality record: one

The apparent simplicity of this type of record sheet does not detract from its usefulness and the fact that only three or four line entries are made is a help rather than a hindrance.

The record is intended as a list of outspoken but confidential comments by a teacher on each child. Such comments can range from 'This child is thoroughly spoiled at home' to 'Jean needs all the love and care she can be given in school'.

These comments are given twice a year, usually about the end of October and the beginning of May. If well maintained throughout a child's primary school career the final document at 10+ shows how a number of teachers have reacted to each child. It should provide a stark outline of each child's basic character.

Such a document is of considerable help to headteachers when they are asked for their advice on the type of secondary education they consider suitable for various children. This is particularly relevant in those areas where 11+ selection has not yet been abolished. Obviously this is not the only record which a headteacher will take into consideration on such occasions, but it usually makes a more realistic assessment of a child's academic potential possible.

General comment

When this record is well maintained in a school it proves invaluable as a method of obtaining a swift résumé of a child's character, needs and problems before talking to parents.

Perhaps one of the main points to stress with teachers who are just about to complete this record for the first time is that they should make their own comments about a child before reading what has been written before. This is quite an obvious requirement as children react to each teacher in a different way and an unbiased opinion is vital.

Fordbury Primary School: Personality record

Surname ..JAMES....... Christian names ..IAN.....

1 Each report should express the teacher's opinion of the child, as it appears to the teacher at the time of the report, irrespective of any other known educational details.

2 Each report must end with the date and teacher's initials.

Ian is a serious little boy who does not play freely with other children. He takes a great interest in anything mathematical.

J. H. Oct 70.

He has become more friendly with other children — especially boys of his own age. Does not seem to mind when he gets hurt playing a rough game

J. H. May 71.

Is reading quite well – helped at home. Has a desire to be better than other children – slightly aggressive.

J. H. Nov 71.

Has suddenly developed a dry sense of humour. He is big for his age. Much less aggressive since he can read well – can be found reading quietly at all times of the day – and night according to his mother.

J. H. May 72

Has settled into this form easily – rather quiet – always polite – enjoys reading.

K. V. Nov 72.

Ian seems to have a desire to be first, or best at everything. He is however popular with other children. Rough at football – fearless in water.

K. V. May 73.

A personality record : two

This type of multichoice record provides the teacher with a solid background of facts from which to fill in the most appropriate square. It is neither difficult to keep nor time wasting to complete, but it makes no allowance for the child who does not really fit into the outline of personal qualities listed.

As a record it appears a little more scientific than the previous record, but it lacks the sparkle of direct personal observation contained within remarks concerning a child's reaction to his environment.

General comment

Despite the clarity of layout the overall assessment of a child is not very easy to grasp. However where the personality factors listed on the left of the record also appear on the local education authority form used when a child transfers to a secondary school, this particular kind of layout can be extremely valuable and time saving. It is the type of record which can be useful to a secondary school when attached to details of a child's academic attainment in the primary school.

Fordbury Primary School : General record card

Age on 1st Sept.1971 ..6 . 4.. Name ..Peter Johns..

Position in family 2 of 4.. Entered present school ..9 – 9 – 70......

	YEARS ONE			TWO			THREE			FOUR		
CAPACITY FOR WORK												
To capacity	■	■	■	■								
Below capacity												
PERSISTENCE												
Very persevering												
Average	■	■	■									
Gives up easily				■								
SPEED OF LEARNING												
Quick	■											
Average		■	■	■								
Very slow												
POWERS OF RETENTION												
Good												
Average	■	■	■	■								
Poor												
TEMPERAMENT												
Easily upset	■	■										
Average			■	■								
Very stable (mature)												
SOCIABILITY (with children)												
Mixes freely				■								
Average			■									
Few friends	■	■										
Solitary												
ATTITUDE TO ADULTS												
Seeks attention	■	■		■								
Friendly			■									
Reserved												
INTERESTS												
Sand and water	■	■	■									
Jigsaws, chess etc				■								
Books				■								
Constructional				■								
Painting and drawing		■		■								
Imaginative play			■									
Sewing, weaving	■											
Music												
Swimming												
Cubs, Brownies												

Teacher's comments ....

....

....

Educational reports for parents

The controversy over the most suitable type of school report to send to a child's parents has gone on so long that it is quite impossible to suggest a form which is even going to remotely satisfy every shade of opinion. Despite this it would be rather cowardly not to make at least one suggestion.

The emphasis on the importance of a child's personal needs in school and the move towards even greater teacher parent cooperation must be reflected in any report which is issued from a school, especially one which uses informal teaching methods. The layout which is illustrated on page 41 reflects these two features of primary school education. First it allows the teacher to comment upon the child's personality at school in approximately the same amount of space that is devoted to academic attainment. Secondly a space is provided for helpful comments by the parents so that they can feel they are contributing towards the well being of their child.

General comment

If printed on thin card these reports can be clipped together with a cheap plastic back binding and kept as a record of each child's yearly progress. ('Bindfast' plastic binding bars are available in various lengths from A. Gill Limited, PO Box 91, Gillmex House, 145 Kensington Road, London SE 11.) This type of report can then be used as an annual report for parents and become a general record of a child's progress since he entered the school.

Fordbury Primary School

Educational report for the parents of Susan Petters

Term ending Summer 1972 Child's age 7:6

Please note that the teacher responsible for this report has been asked to comment upon those aspects of your child's character which are above or below average. Where a report is brief you may assume that your child is making a satisfactory and normal progress through the school.

Social behaviour : health, intelligence, imagination, interests, emotions, sociability.

Although small for her age Susan is developing into a forceful character. She is above average in general intelligence and has many friends including some older than herself. She is very self reliant and appears to have an unusally wide knowledge of horses, riding and stable work.

Academic subjects: reading, mathematics, drama, art, music, sports.

Above average progress has been made in all subjects. Susan has been particularly quick to read music and play a recorder. Academically good. Since learning to swim two months ago she has now swum 100 metres in a good style of breastroke.

This report was written by Mrs V. Smith. on 10th July 72.

Parent's comments This report should be returned to school by .... and if you feel you have any comments which will add to our knowledge of your child would you please be kind enough to write them below.

Susan loves swimming but often complains of headaches and earaches afterwards

Signed J. Petters (Parent)

To help our school records, will you please let us have a telephone number where you can be contacted during the daytime Hertford 941

This school reassembles on 9th September 1972

Headteacher's initials L.D.

The data card system

The basic principle of the data card system is that when a hole is left complete on a card it indicates that the information associated with that hole is valid for the child concerned. When a hole is opened up the information does not apply. Obviously it is the teacher's task to cut open those holes which do not refer to the child for whom she is completing a card.

By keeping the data cards together in such a way that a thin knitting needle can be threaded through the holes, every child with similar characteristics can be extracted from the complete set of cards. (See illustration on page 44.) So if a teacher threads a knitting needle through a complete set of data cards by passing it down the line of 'Only child in the family' holes, she will be able to lift out all the cards for children without sisters or brothers. All the cards left in the set will refer to families of two or more children.

With this system the layout of the data card and the information a teacher wishes to record are a matter of personal choice. The example on page 43 shows a two sided data card whose holes refer only to the information contained on the front of the card. If such cards are made square they will fit sideways into the box in which they are kept. This means two more holes, one per side, can be added to those at the top and bottom.

All together the layout shown can provide a choice of sixteen pieces of positive or negative information on the front of the card plus space for three additional types of information on the back. Each card is designed to last for a period of two years. The first year is indicated by a large letter A in the top left hand corner and the second by a B in the opposite corner.

Examples of data cards

Joan Lormer

Page 45 JOAN LORMER shows how the front of the data card is filled in for a girl of low intelligence, aged 7·5 years, with no brothers or sisters, who is in poor health and solitary by nature.

John Game

Page 45 JOHN GAME shows how the card of a boy of average intelligence, aged 7·3 years on September 1st, with no brothers or sisters, who is a sociable child despite poor health, would be filled in.

It should be noted that when John reaches the age of 8·3 years, he is no longer in poor health and can be regarded as a child with no outstanding problems or achievements.

Fordbury Primary School : Holed data card for general record of child

Front

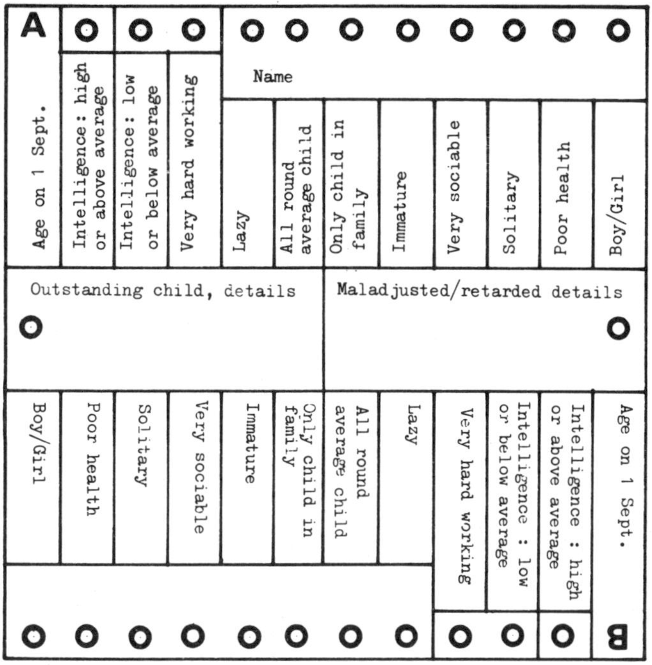

Back

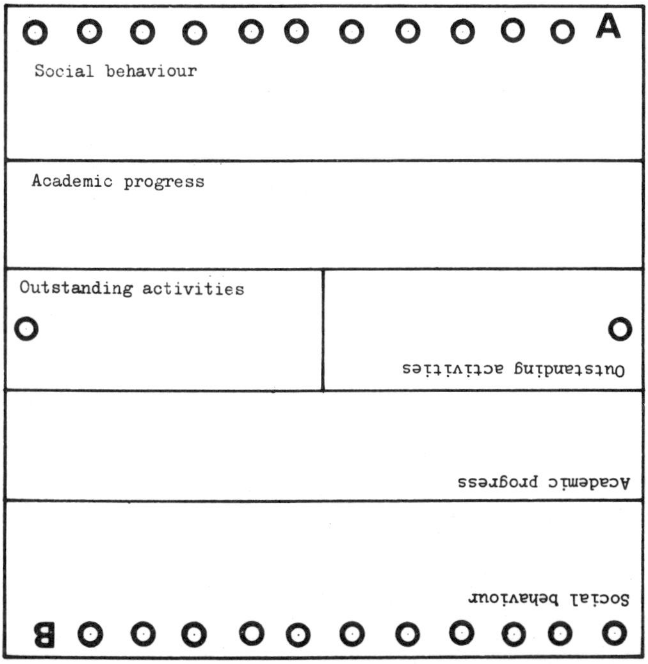

Size of card 100 mm x 100 mm

Card 4 sheet thickness

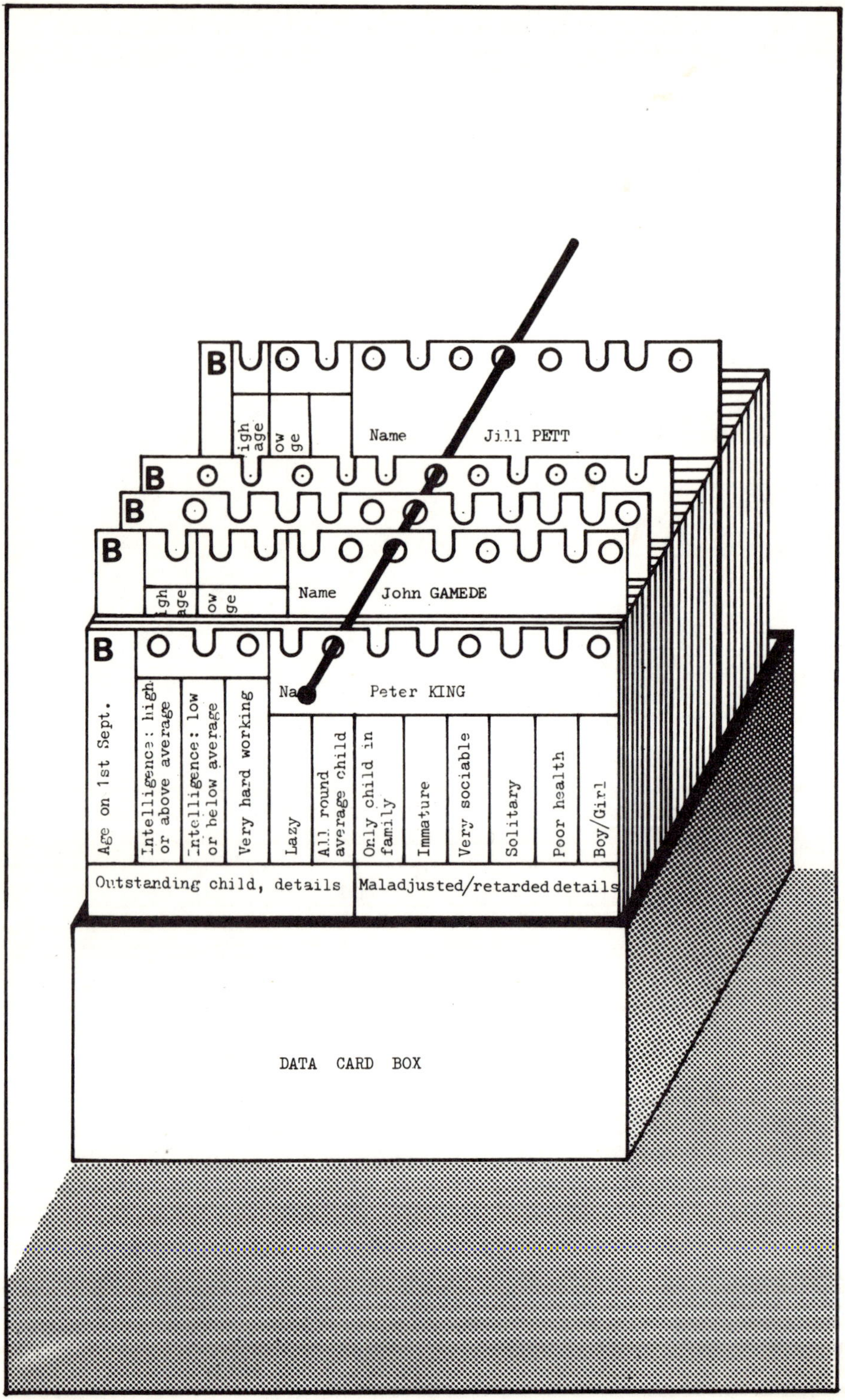
B
Name Jill PETT
B
B
B
Name John GAMEDE
B
Name Peter KING
Age on 1st Sept.
Intelligence: high or above average
Intelligence: low or below average
Very hard working
Lazy
All round average child
Only child in family
Immature
Very sociable
Solitary
Poor health
Boy/Girl
Outstanding child, details
Maladjusted/retarded details
DATA CARD BOX

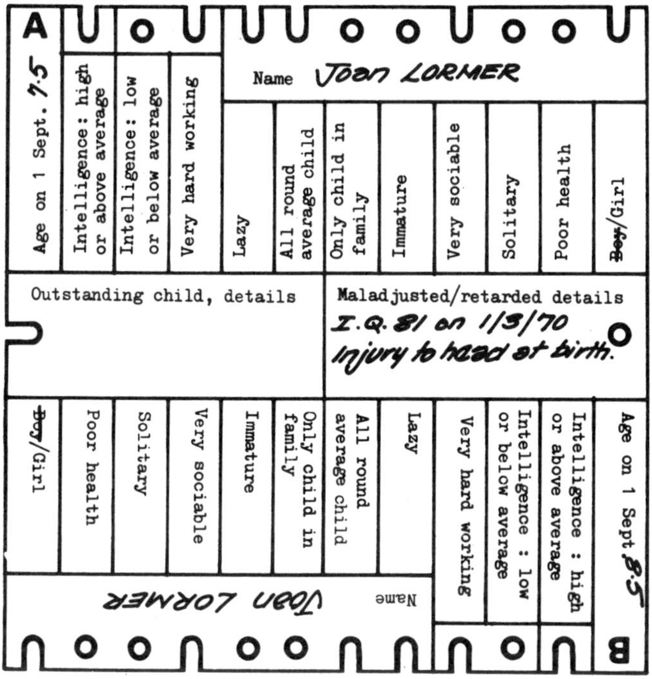
A
Age on 1 Sept. 7.5
Intelligence: high or above average
Intelligence: low or below average
Very hard working
Name Joan LORMER
Lazy
All round average child
Only child in family
Immature
Very sociable
Solitary
Poor health
Boy/Girl
Outstanding child, details
Maladjusted/retarded details
I.Q. 81 on 1/3/70
Injury to head at birth.
Boy/Girl
Poor health
Solitary
Very sociable
Immature
Only child in family
All round average child
Lazy
Very hard working
Intelligence : low or below average
Intelligence : high or above average
Age on 1 Sept 8.5
Name Joan LORMER
B

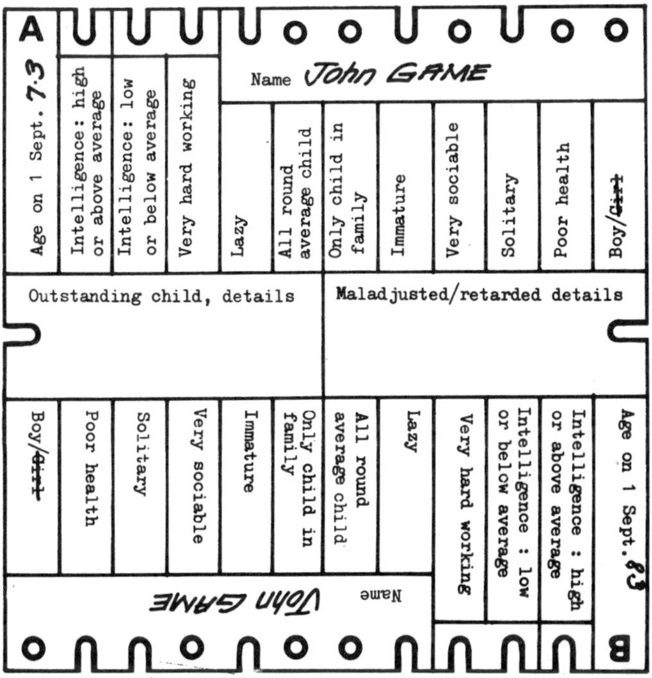
A
Age on 1 Sept. 7.3
Intelligence: high or above average
Intelligence: low or below average
Very hard working
Name John GAME
Lazy
All round average child
Only child in family
Immature
Very sociable
Solitary
Poor health
Boy/Girl
Outstanding child, details
Maladjusted/retarded details
Boy/Girl
Poor health
Solitary
Very sociable
Immature
Only child in family
All round average child
Lazy
Very hard working
Intelligence : low or below average
Intelligence : high or above average
Age on 1 Sept. 8.3
Name John GAME
B

A teacher's record of the integrated day

The method of recording shown on page 47 reveals a child's progress in the four main areas of school activity, i.e. mathematics, English, art and craft and other activities such as games, swimming, music, science, French, religion. It also shows what sort of balance has been maintained between these subjects over a period of six weeks. If informal teaching methods are employed it is essential that each child should have a well balanced experience of each subject.

Record keeping consists of filling in four daily segments of a weekly pie diagram for each child in the group. The teacher will have a folder containing one sheet for each child and the daily record is made by filling in a fraction of each of the four segments. Each segment represents one day's work so the extent to which the teacher fills in the segment indicates how much of the school day the child has spent working on the subject. The time taken by the teacher to complete the record is reasonable and works out at approximately one minute per child.

Obviously to make the record effective the teacher has to remember how each child spent the day. If a teacher cannot recall what a child has been doing, she should make a point of finding out when the child returns to school next day. This record must be filled in neatly if the end product is to be easily read.

Once completed each pie diagram immediately reveals the educational balance of each child's activities. For example, the illustration given shows Week 1 to have been a well balanced week. Week 2 shows an over emphasis on both mathematics and art, while Week 3 reveals a considerable concentration on art. The child was absent on Monday of Week 4 and had a low output of work for the whole week. Very little English was done during Weeks 2, 3 and 4 but Week 5 shows a considerable bias towards English because the teacher spoke to the child about the lack of work in this subject area. Finally Week 6 shows an uncompleted pie diagram.

General comment

The usefulness of this record is in direct proportion to the enthusiasm with which the teacher maintains it. If well maintained it provides an excellent indication of each child's daily activities over a period of about half a term. As only six such sheets will cover almost a year it is easy to build up a visual display of how a child has worked over considerable lengths of time.

On first sight this method may seem difficult to understand and interpret. Once mastered however it becomes very meaningful and useful conclusions can be quickly drawn from it, such as the effect of an absence on following work or the lack of work before a prolonged absence due to illness.

Fordbury Primary School:Activity record

Date record started 7.9.71.... Name Peter Holmes....

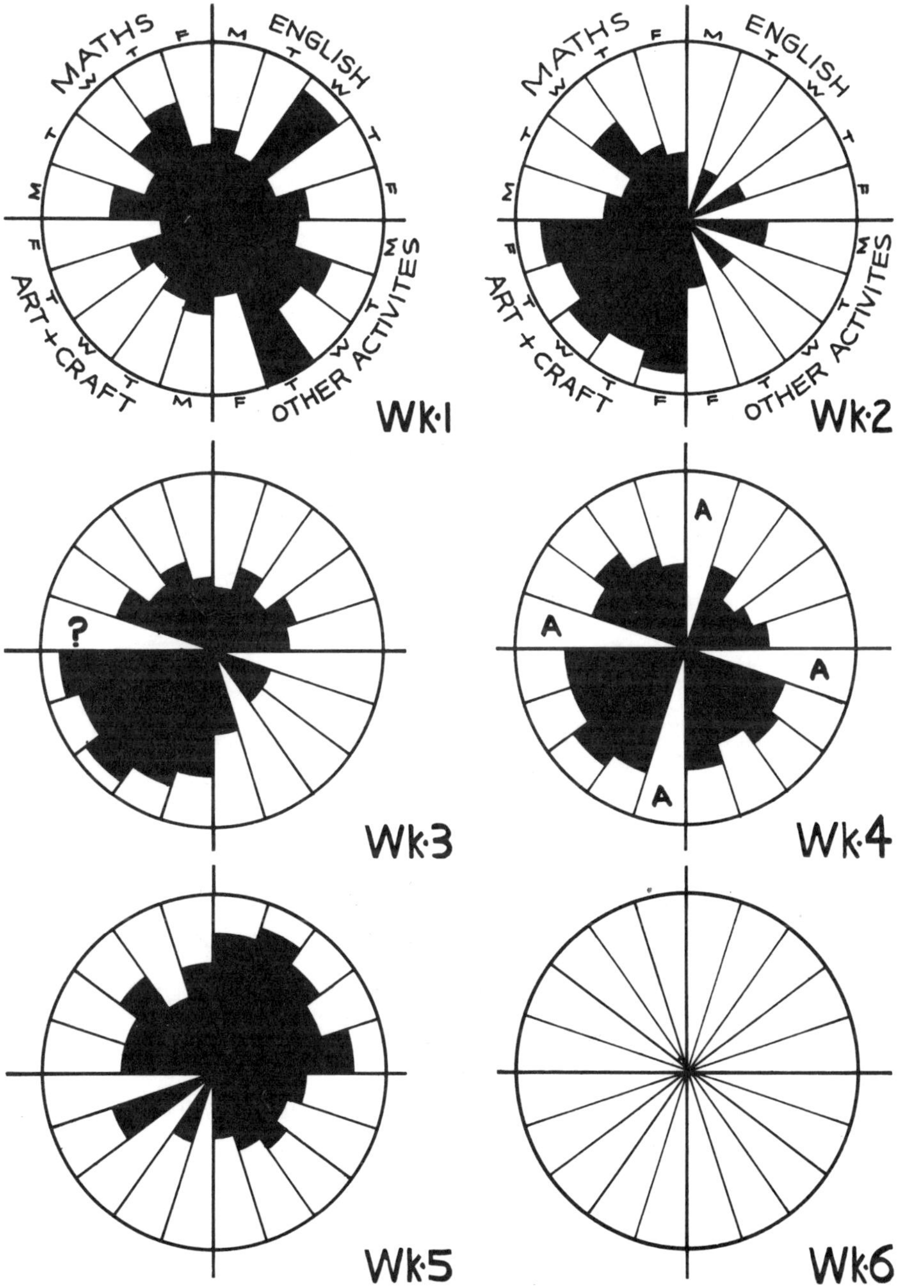

Teachers should assess balance of child's education and comment over the page.

A teacher's record of activity work

This record may be kept separately from a child's record or attached to the reverse of the child's record if required. All entries should be dated and initialed.

Week 1

Peter has worked well this week.

J. H. Jan 9th 70.

Week 2

A great deal has been learned from constructing a model of a local clock tower. This has involved timekeeping measurements scale drawings, finding heights of tall objects.

J. H. Jan 16th 70.

Week 3

Model tower construction has taken up a great deal of time - little English or maths J.H. Jan 23rd 70

Week 4

Absent for blood test at hospital. An average weeks work but still not much written English. Have made some suggestions.

J.H. Jan 30th 70.

Week 5

Poetry and play writing leading to mime – all connected with the ghost of the clock tower. Music on handbells composed

J.H. Feb 6th 70

Week ....

....

....

....

This is sheet number ....

A child's record of the integrated day

One solution to the problem of recording the diverse activities of over thirty children working in an integrated situation at the upper end of the primary school is to make each child responsible for maintaining his own work record.

There is no legitimate reason why this cannot be done, provided that such records are supervised by a teacher. If well organized this type of record will enable a teacher to see that each child makes a well balanced contact with all the subjects he should study over a period of a week or more. It is possible to obtain an immediate indication of the daily balance of basic subjects from the fact than an A, B, and C appear among the subject abbreviations listed for each day. The numbers associated with these letters will indicate the exact nature of the work undertaken. The space provided for the teacher's comments can be used for any remarks she wants to make about the child's progress over the course of a week.

General comment

The record sheet shown is simple enough for any child to use effectively, and by using only four sheets it is possible for a teacher to have a daily record of a child over the major part of a school term. However, it is essentially a record of what has happened in the immediate past and is not very successful in showing how a child has developed over the course of a year.

Informal teaching techniques place great emphasis on the needs and responsibilities of the individual child, so it is quite natural that each child should be expected to record his own progress. There is no advantage to be gained from falsifying such a record and this rarely happens. A similar record to the one suggested on page 50 has in fact proved to be both workable and informative in an informal school when backed by the teacher's own record.

Sheet number ....

Fordbury Primary School

This is the work record of ..Joan Lane..........

I started this on Jan. 17 My teacher is Miss Jones

Only use the abbreviations when filling in your daily record.

English	Reading	A1	Maths	Practical work	B1
	Writing	A2		Written work	B2
	Mime	A3		Text book	B3
	Drama	A4		Maths with teacher (formal)	B4
	Speech (reading aloud)	A5			
Art and Craft	Painting or drawing	C1	Other Subjects	Educational visit	EV
	Handwork or models	C2		Games e.g. cricket	G
	Plasticine or clay	C3		Swimming	S
				Music	M
				French	F
				Science	Sc
				Religion	R

Day	Week .1..	Week	Week ....
Monday	A1 A2 B1 B4 C1 M		
Tuesday	F S A4 B1 B4 C1 F		
Wednesday	A1 A4 B2 M R G		
Thursday	E V C2		
Friday	A1 A2 B3 F R		

Teacher's comments (with initials and date)

..12 girls visted local farm for a........
..morning on Thursday 20th Jan..........
..Start of a study on cows............SJ. Jan 21.
....
....

Recording a class activity

The record sheet lists the main features of this type of activity at the head of each column and it is maintained simply by filling in each stage of the work as it is completed. A note of the date upon which each stage was finished will be found useful when an assessment has to be made of what has been achieved.

In every case the column headings—Introduction, Collecting information, Research, Collation, End product, Digestion and storage—provide an outline of natural progression which can be completed or ignored if not relevant to the task in hand.

In industry this type of record is regarded as a simple form of flow diagram and when used as such teachers will find it extremely instructive.

General comment

Not every class activity should be recorded in this manner but where a teaching technique is used for the first time or an activity is new to a teacher, it is often useful to know how long each stage took. The diagram will also act as a reminder of the various facets of this type of work which require careful planning and as a skeleton showing the natural order into which these teaching techniques seem to divide themselves.

Students find such records very useful when planning, preparing and coordinating their work in school. They are also very instructive to tutors who want to discover the rate of progress achieved by a student on teaching practice.

A group of teachers engaged in team teaching will find a chart of this nature invaluable as a means of coordinating their activities.

TITLE *Paper Making Project*

PROGRESS RECORD OF A PROJECT OR TOPIC

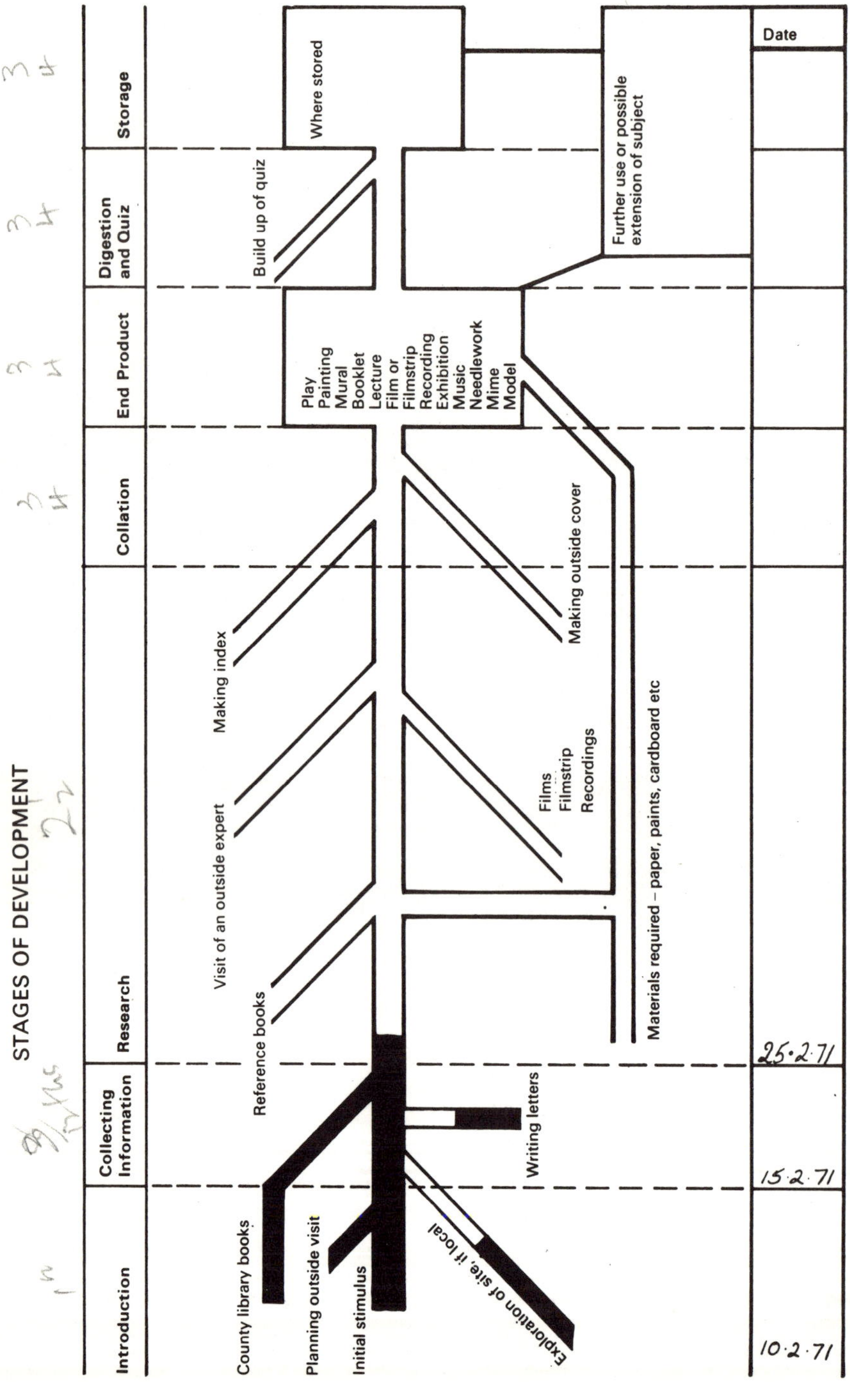

A reading progress record: one

There are occasions when a teacher wishes to record a child's progress in a particular academic subject in the primary school. This is especially true of the basic skills to be mastered in mathematics and learning to read and write.

The reading record shown on page 54 is maintained by the teacher who fills in the date when a particular reading book is completed. In addition a dated list of comments is maintained on the reverse side of the sheet. Such a record is easy to keep even in a busy infant classroom and should be completed as each child reaches the end of every stage of his reading development.

Three separate reading schemes have been listed side by side and each child will work through them in whatever way best suits his own requirements. Although this has proved an excellent method of teaching reading, it does demand that the teacher has a thorough grasp of the reading schemes used so that she can match each child's needs with the scheme most likely to satisfy them. For example the record illustrated shows that the child read every book at stage two of each scheme because the teacher felt that extra reinforcement of the reading techniques associated with this stage was needed.

No record is shown for any child who has completed the scheme successfully; if a child can read well there is little point in recording this fact by listing a continuous string of books he or she has read.

General comment

Obviously the important aspects of this record are the general layout and the fact that it can be applied to any number of reading schemes other than those shown on the example.

The inclusion of the date the child entered the school has been found to be of very practical importance when a child's progress is being assessed. It is particularly relevant where a child has transferred from another school in the middle of learning to read.

The layout on the reverse side of this record will prove very useful in those cases where reading difficulties arise.

Fordbury Primary School : Infants reading record

Date of entry : 13 Nov 77 Name Susan King

Date of birth : 6 Nov 72

Any physical problems : Weak left eye

JANET AND JOHN	MCKEE	BEACON
Here We Go .... Janet and John 1 .... Off to Play 17.2.78 21.3.78	Tip 21.3.78 4.5.78	
Out and About Janet and John 2 9.10.78 20.11.78	Tip and Mitten 4.5.78 6.7.78	Old Dog Tom 6.7.78 9.10.78 Little Chick Chick ....
Janet and John 3 13.2.79 2.4.79	With Peter and Susan	Pancake 20.11.78 16.7.79
Janet and John 4 16.7.79 12.9.79	Up and Away	Careful Hans 2.4.79 16.7.79
Once Upon a Time	On We Go	Briar Rose 12.9.79 11.12.79
		Seven Proud Sisters 11.12.79 .... William Tell ....

Reading progress record: Part two

Date	Name of test	CA	RA	Standard score	Teacher's initials
9.10.72	Holborn	6.9	7.8	113	J.R.

Assessment of reading skills

This assessment may be made in note form or by using a five point scale as follows a = excellent b = good c = average d = below average e = very poor

Sight Left eye..............Right eye..................

Hearing Left ear.............Right ear..................

Speech..

....

Stage of language development at 7 years................

....

Writing hand Left/right Ability to coordinate hand and eye...

....

Phonic readiness.....................................

Ability to concentrate................................

....

Teacher's comments (with date and initials)

....

....

....

....

....

....

....

....

....

A reading progress record: two

This reading record is very similar to the previous record except that it lists other commonly known reading schemes. These have been arranged (and the layout designed) so that each stage contains books of a similar standard of reading difficulty. A child is not expected to read every book listed but rather to thread his way through each stage according to his personal needs.

General comment

Once the child has completed the basic ita reading course this method of recording a child's progress in reading can be applied.

Well known reading schemes have been used to illustrate the layout of both this and the previous record, but it is the method of constructing this type of record which is important and not the reading schemes employed to illustrate it. Other schemes which could be similarly employed are *Through the Rainbow* (Schofield and Sims), *Oxford Colour Reading* books (OUP), *Happy Venture* (Oliver and Boyd), *Time for Reading* (Ginn).

Fordbury Primary School : General reading record

Date of entry .... Class .... Name ....

STAGE ONE	Date completed
Janet and John 1 'Off to Play'	______
Beacon 'Old Friends'	______
'Toys at Play'	______
Happy Venture 1	______
Ladybird Book 2a : Ladybird 2b	______
Janet and John 'Out and About'	______
STAGE TWO	
Janet and John 2 'We Went Walking'	______
Beacon Readers 2	______
Happy Venture 2	______
Ladybird 3a : Ladybird 3b	______
Ladybird 4a : Ladybird 4b	______
STAGE THREE	
Janet and John 3 'Through the Garden Gate'	______
Beacon Readers 3	______
Happy Venture 3	______
Ladybird 5a : Ladybird 5b	______
Ladybird 6a : Ladybird 6b	______
STAGE FOUR	
Janet and John 4 'I Know a Story'	______
Beacon Readers 4	______
Happy Venture 4	______
Ladybird 7a : Ladybird 7b	______
STAGE FIVE	
Janet and John 5 'Once Upon a Time'	______
Beacon Readers 5	______
Ladybird 8a : Ladybird 8b	______
Ladybird 9a : Ladybird 9b	______
STAGE SIX	
'High on a Hill'	______
Beacon Readers 6	______
Beacon 'Friendly Tales'	______
Wide Range 1	______
Ladybird 10a : Ladybird 10b	______
Wide Range 2	______
Ladybird 11a : Ladybird 11b	______
Wide Range 3	______
Ladybird 12a : Ladybird 12b	______
'It Must be Magic'	______
Wide Range 4	______
'Magic Everywhere'	______
Wide Range 5	______
'Over the Sea'	______
Wide Range 6	______

General comments (Please give date and initials by each comment)

....
....
....

A reading workshop record sheet

This particular record sheet is designed for use with a reading workshop such as the one published by Ward Lock Educational or Science Research Associates Reading Laboratory, and should be completed by the child as he works his way through a reading workshop.

It has some interesting features. First, the child becomes responsible for any assessment and criticism of what has been achieved. Open ended statements such as, 'Underline how many marks you would give yourself for this work' and 'Why did you not give yourself more marks?' all enhance the 'self help' concept of the workshop approach to learning. Second, the questions concerning time provide a concrete link with mathematics and other kinds of record keeping for the child. Third, most teachers who have used a workshop for improving reading standards find that the children become enthusiastic about recording their own achievements and are remarkably honest when marking or assessing their own work.

General comment

Obviously this record sheet has been designed to meet the specific needs of the workshops mentioned above, but its general concept can be easily applied to other reading workshops.

Once the record sheet has been completed by the child it should be kept for a while in his personal file.

A reading workshop record sheet

Reading card .... Date ....

Write your name here ....

What colour card are you using? .... Which number? ...

Keep a record of the time you take to finish this card.

Started .... hrs .... mins. Finished .... hrs .... mins.

Started .... hrs .... mins. Finished .... hrs .... mins.

Fill in your answers on the lines below

1 .... 16 ....

2 .... 17 ....

3 .... 18 ....

4 .... 19 ....

5 .... 20 ....

6 .... 21 ....

7 .... 22 ....

8 .... 23 ....

9 .... 24 ....

10 .... 25 ....

11 .... 26 ....

12 .... 27 ....

13 .... 28 ....

14 .... 29 ....

15 .... 30 ....

Write here the date you finished this card ....

How many hours and minutes did this colour card take you?
.... hrs ...... mins.

How many answers did you get right? .... wrong?......

Underline how many marks you would give yourself for this work

1 2 3 4 5 6 7 8 9 10

Why did you not give yourself more marks? ....

....

Make a list of all your wrong answers here ....

.... and find out where you went wrong.

Show this sheet to your teacher and then put it in your personal file before your forget.

An infant school mathematics record

This mathematics record is very similar to the reading record shown earlier in so far as it is kept by the teacher who fills in the date when each piece of work is completed by the child.

The layout of the record illustrated is designed to be used in an informal mathematics environment within a school using the 'family grouping' method of organization.

General comment

There is nothing particularly unusual about this record sheet except that it provides space for notes concerning work which is undertaken but not provided for on the typed list.

Fordbury Primary School : Mathematics record

Date of birth 23-6-68 Child's name Joan Jones

General remarks Group 3 (Family Grouping)

Group	Formal work	Practical work
1	Introduction to numbers 10.10.73 Drawing round numbers 20.9.73 Placing objects beside numbers Using number apparatus 14.10.73	Verses, jingles, poems of numbers 9.9.73 Number games – card grouping 10.10.73 – being numbers 20.9.73 – fetching numbers
2	Writing numbers 1 to 10 6.12.73 Picture and practical – addition 10.1.74 – subtraction Book First Steps in Numbers Book 1	As for Group 1, plus Scoring games, dice, nine pins, fish numbers, hoop-la } 15.1.74 Free shop play Knowledge of shapes, sizes, etc
3	Numbers 1 to 20 Addition tables Formal tens and units } 30.2.74 Addition and subtraction Pence, Pounds Tables 2 x , 3 x Book	Make cardboard ruler Cardboard clock Scoring games Plays about a shop Capacity measuring play Division games in P E
4	Numbers 1 to 100 Tables 4 x , 5 x Multiplication, simple division Time Money plus, minus Word problems Revision	Clocks Guided shop play Guided capacity work with sand and water Time – days, months, seasons ....

Remarks (with date) as to progress

25.11.73 Double numbers often written backwards. Work was very untidy but improved since I stopped the use of a rubber

30.2.74 Her work is much tidier – ready for + and –

Group	Formal work	Practical work
5	Revision T U +, −, x ÷ Tables 2 x, 3 x, 4 x, 5 x Money x, division Simple problems Book	Measuring, weighing in handicraft Time – poems of seasons, names, spellings of days, months Number games ....
6	4 Rules up to T U Tables 2 x to 6 x or more Money +, −, x, ÷ (with carrying) Problems T U Distance +, −, cm, metres, km, Weight +, −, gm, kg Use of $\frac{1}{2}$, $\frac{1}{4}$, $\frac{1}{8}$ Book	Practical $\frac{1}{2}$, $\frac{1}{4}$, $\frac{1}{8}$ Practical measuring in cm, m Some formal re-inforcement of morning work if required ....

Remarks (with date) as to progress

____

____

____

____

____

____

NB The details shown on this record are not intended as a syllabus.

Recording assignment cards used in infant mathematics schemes

The record sheet on page 64 is designed to cope with a very informal classroom situation. The children use individual assignment cards for various branches of mathematics under the general direction of the teacher.

Each child is allowed to choose one of the seven mathematical subjects listed on the record sheet. Having chosen one, say length, a child has to start with the first red assignment card and proceed along the red path (cards 1 to 10) as far as he wishes. If a child becomes bored with length, or is finding the work too difficult, he moves on to another mathematical subject, such as money, provided that he also starts on the red coloured cards in this subject.

The main feature of this scheme is that a child cannot proceed to stage two of the work (buff coloured cards) until he has completed every red card available in all the subject areas. So, although a child can proceed in any order, he has to cover all subject areas before he can move on to the next stage in any of them. The reverse side of this record sheet has proved of great assistance to lower junior school teachers when the children have just arrived from the infant school.

General comment

Obviously the record card illustrated on page 64 is designed to fit one specific set of assignment cards but the basic principle of this scheme and its colour system is applicable to nearly all assignment cards.

The record can be maintained by either the teacher or the children provided that the individual cards are kept readily available in a folder and that each child is trained to fill in his record after completing each assignment.

Fordbury Primary School : Infant assignment card mathematics record

Child entered class on ..5.1.71.. Name ..John Smith..

Progressive assignment cards in order

Subject	Colour	Number	1	2	3	4	5	6	7	8	9	10
LENGTH	Red	1										
	Buff	2										
	Yellow	3										
	White	4										
	Spare	5										
WEIGHT	Red	1										
	Buff	2										
	Yellow	3										
	White	4										
	Spare	5										
CAPACITY	Red	1										
	Buff	2										
	Yellow	3										
	White	4										
	Spare	5										
MONEY	Red	1										
	Buff	2										
	Yellow	3										
	White	4										
	Spare	5										
TIME	Red	1										
	Buff	2										
	Yellow	3										
	White	4										
	Spare	5										
FRACTIONS	Red	1										
	Buff	2										
	Yellow	3										
	White	4										
	Spare	5										
AREA and VOLUME	Red	1										
	Buff	2										
	Yellow	3										
	White	4										
	Spare	5										

Teacher's comments

22.2.71 Shows great interest in length. 15.3.71 Good money sense of values 10.5.71 All red cards completed.

An infant school mathematics record : Part two

COMPUTATION

	Free play	Box 10	Box 9	Box 8	Box 7	Box 6	Box 5
Stern apparatus	2.2.71						

Box 4	Box 3

Number bonds of :	5	6	7	8	9	10	Book 1
							Started .... Ended ....

Number bonds of :	11	12	13	14	15	16	17	18	19	20

+ and - x and ÷

Book 2 Book 3

Started .... Ended .... Started .... Ended ....

Tens and units card	+	-	x	÷	Tables	2	3	4	5	6	7	8	9

+ and - x and ÷

Book 4 Book 5

Started .... Ended .... Started .... Ended ....

Teacher's comments

Mathematics record : one

The record sheet illustrated on page 67 is designed to list all source material on certain mathematical topics which may be covered during a particular period of time.

First it is important to note that it is *not* intended that a child should work his way slowly down the record sheet, although such sheets may be graded so that he tends to move in that general direction. The sequence of work will be indicated by the teacher filling in the date when work is completed. The right hand list of general contents will provide an easy reference for seeing what subjects have been covered. The left hand columns indicate where additional textbook material can be found if required.

The drawback to this particular type of record is that it can degenerate into a convenient but thoughtless method for teaching mathematics.

General comment

This is a very flexible method of recording if correctly used. The back of the sheet provides space for recording what mathematics have been undertaken as a result of discovery lessons or as part of a project. Such flexibility is made possible by the fact that no record is kept of the teaching technique employed to teach a child a specific mathematical concept.

The example given is intended as an illustration of how part of a record might be compiled for a lower junior class. If necessary each sheet can be given a different colour as the child progresses up the school.

Fordbury Primary School : Mathematics record : one

Date of birth .... Child's name ....

Previous teacher .... Date entered school ....

Item Revision cards	Book	Pages	Date	General contents + − x ÷ Mechanical and problem
Long division	Maths 1	13 - 46		T U Odd and even numbers
Fractions	Beta 1 (1969) L E M 2 Maths 1	12 - 15 72 - 7 49 - 50		+ - Complete numbers, $\frac{1}{2}$, $\frac{1}{4}$ 1 $\frac{1}{2}$ $\frac{1}{4}$ $\frac{1}{8}$ $\frac{1}{3}$ + - $\frac{1}{2}$ $\frac{1}{4}$ $\frac{1}{8}$ + -
Money	Beta 1(1969) L E M (Metric)	4 - 5 7 - 10 16 - 17 32 - 35 47 65 - 66 6 - 17		Coins 10p 5p 2p 1p + - up to 20 $\frac{1}{2}$p using coins £1 and coins, giving change + - x ÷ General use of coins
Length	L E M 1 Beta 1 (1969) L E M 2	82 - 86 22 - 23 38 - 39 24 - 26 91 - 92		Measuring pacing span foot Lines Metric measures m, cm Personal measurements
Shapes and Angles	Beta 1 (1969)	38 - 41 53 - 55 60 - 63 75 - 76		Lines, right angles 3 D shapes Square, rectangle, circle Patterns, shapes and space
Area	L E M 2	22 - 29		Measuring area, using geo-boards
Time	Beta 1(1969) L E M 2 Maths 1	18 - 19 44 - 45 74 78 - 83 76 - 82		Telling time, clocks, etc The calendar Revision Telling the time Telling the time
Block graphs	Beta 1 (1969) L E M 2	21 - 22 30 - 31 84 - 85		
Capacity	Beta 1 (1969)	56 - 57 72 - 73		Metric measures, litre, $\frac{1}{2}$ litre Metric revision
Weight	L E M (Metric) Beta 1 (1969)	42 50 - 52		Measuring weight Metric measures kg, $\frac{1}{2}$ kg

All practical mathematics will be recorded on a separate Discovery Work record

Note for teachers

1 The books and references shown above are included solely as a means of illustrating the layo this type of record and have no connection with any scheme of work.

2 The Discovery Work record can be found on page 73 .

<u>Mathematics record : one</u>

Name of child ....

Teacher's remarks

Teachers are requested to note the child's difficulties with mathematics. Each entry should be initialed and dated.

Date	Comments	Initials

Mathematics record: two

This record is similar to the previous example except that in this case the child is expected to maintain it himself. A space is provided in which the books which the child has used to gain a greater understanding of a mathematical concept can be noted. By including both 'start' and 'finish' dates on the record, the teacher will be able to equate the amount of time used with the difficulty or size of the task undertaken. Any mathematical textbook used by the children should be carefully revised by the teacher beforehand so that time wasting exercises devoted to the mechanical repetition of certain processes are removed.

General comment

Although this record layout is suitable for upper juniors, it will not be entirely based on textbooks as a great deal of practical work should be undertaken. Indeed the front and the back of this record combined are capable of recording a child's mathematical progress regardless of the form his work takes.

Fordbury Primary School : Mathematics record : two

Name of child ....

Teacher's remarks

Teachers may either comment on difficulties encountered, or record by **date and subject** the order in which they helped the child carry out the work.

Date	Comments	Initials

Note for teachers

As with all previous maths records shown in this book, the details of subjects and textbooks quoted [do] not represent a scheme of work and are there solely as a means of illustrating the layout of this meth[od] of keeping a record.

Fordbury Primary School : Mathematics record : two

Date entered school or class ....

Name of child ....

Mathematical subject	Date Start	Date Finish
1 Revision of tables 0x to 12x		
2 Revision of H T U in + -		
3 Revision of T U in x ÷		
4 Revision decimals + - x ÷		
5 Revision fractions + - x ÷		
6 Percentages, decimal, fraction, relationships		
7 Area by formula L x B, $\frac{1}{2}$ ht. x base, πr^2		
8 Volume formula ht. x L x B		
9 Decimal coinage		
10 Metric measurement, area, volume		
11 Use of scales, plans, maps		
12 Bearings, time, distance		
13 Spirals and concentric circles		
14 Metric weights, capacity		
15 Astronomical numbers		
16 Calculation of heights		
17 Levers and proportion		
18 Properties and 3 D shapes		
19 Properties and use of the pendulum		
20 Algebra (simple problems)		
21 Practical geometry and survey		
22 Use of slide rules + ÷ x		
23 Changing bases. Use of formula $x^5, x^4, x^3, x^2, x^1, x^0$		

Make a list of titles of individual mathematical subjects studied, individual books or work cards used.

List work from general maths textbooks with contents revised by teacher	Pages	Start	Finish

A discovery or activity record sheet

The layout of this record is extremely simple but very effective as it can be applied to a wide range of subjects including discovery mathematics.

The progress of each piece of work is indicated by the teacher or child who makes a few notes (with dates) when the work reaches certain important stages.

General comment

Provided no attempt is made to keep an elaborate and detailed record, one or two sheets should cover at least a term's work, hence the choice of terms provided at the top of the sheet. The space for recording books will enable quick reference to be made to them as the work proceeds and act as an indication of which books have been taken from the school library.

Fordbury Primary School : Discovery and activity record sheet

Name of child Vera Smith. Joan Green. Doreen Inns

Term 1, 2 ✓, 3 (please tick term concerned) Year 1971

Details of subject	Books used	Start	Finish
Vera Smith, Joan Green and Doreen Inns, are studying Vera's new home – ELizabethan cottage. 6 Feb.	General collection from school library.		
Elizabethan dresses, cost of food and clothes and amusements being studied 13 Feb	History of Everyday Things. Vol 2 The Seven Queens of England	Feb 1 Feb	Mar 9 Feb
Large 20 page folder, dolls in period costume, collection of Elizabethan games put to mime. Shakespeare 'discovered' 19 Feb	Copy of Merchant of Venice' England Book 3	12 Feb	28 Feb
Attempts to write poetry as per Shakespeare. Vera enjoyed simple prose copy of M. of Venice Copy of 'Greensleeves' music tried on recorder 22 Feb.	My own copy of M. of Venice from home William Shakespeare by Ivor Brown.	20 Feb	10 Mar
Small display of work completed – drawings – mime of play and games for remainder of class. Three Elizabethan prayers for morning assembly read by group. End of activity 24 Feb			

Recording achievement on standardized tests

The record sheet illustrated has been compiled for use with the wide range of standardized tests available and shows how such results can be correlated. As the basic average score for nearly all these tests is 100 such a layout is very adaptable.

The inclusion of a column for any IQ (intelligence quotient) scores is not essential and this figure must not be included when finding a child's EQ (educational quotient). A record of the child's chronological age at the time a test was taken is vital.

The EQ is found by averaging out the achievement scores obtained in columns 3 to 7. The remarks column provided can be used to record the teacher's assessment of the child on a five point scale (A to E), if required.

General comment

This is perhaps the most simple yet the most relevant record which can be maintained for primary school children as it deals with concrete facts and allows a detailed comparison to be made between children. For example such a record allows comparisons to be made between the achievement of a child in a school ten years ago and a child in a school at present.

Unless an academic test has been scientifically standardized, it seems quite pointless to keep a record of results in order to compare one child with another because any academic test compiled within the bounds of even a large school will invariably produce a curve of distribution which is nowhere near the correct one for the country as a whole.

Standardized tests are not the only method of academic assessment but they do eliminate many problems when a child's progress is recorded annually, and this is the reason why further uses for them are suggested on the following pages.

Fordbury Primary School : Record of achievement on standardized tests 1971. to 1976

Name of child	Chronological age at time of test	Intelligence quotient	Verbal reading quotient	Spelling quotient	Study skills quotient	English quotient	Mathematical quotient	Educational quotient	General remarks
John SMITH	6.5		93	85	101	96	99	93	In hospital two months before tests
	7.5		108	99	102	98	103	102	
	8.6	109	108	98	101	100	109	103	
	9.5		109	99	104	99	110	104	
	10.5	112	112	104	110	105	108	108	
Joy HILL	6.4		108	106	110	112	115	110	
	7.4	120	115	112	115	109	117	113	
	8.5		117	113	120	115	117	117	
	9.4	135	119	118	119	113	120	118	
	10.4		125	121	127	118	123	123	
Peter PARKS	6.0		85	80	81	84	82	83	
	7.0	92	A	A	A	83	85	84	
	8.1		87	81	80	87	90	85	
	9.0	93	89	83	A	93	A	88	
	10.0		88	84	83	89	91	87	
Rose GREEN	6.3		138	135	117	109	108	121	
	7.4	137	125	121	145	125	112	126	
	8.3		125	120	129	107	115	119	
	9.3	133	128	104	124	104	126	119	
	10.4		140	124	126	123	103	123	

Fordbury Primary School : Graphical form of record card for standardized attainment tests

Previous school if any ....

Name of child Joan Lay.

Date entered school 9:9:70

Date graph started 1972

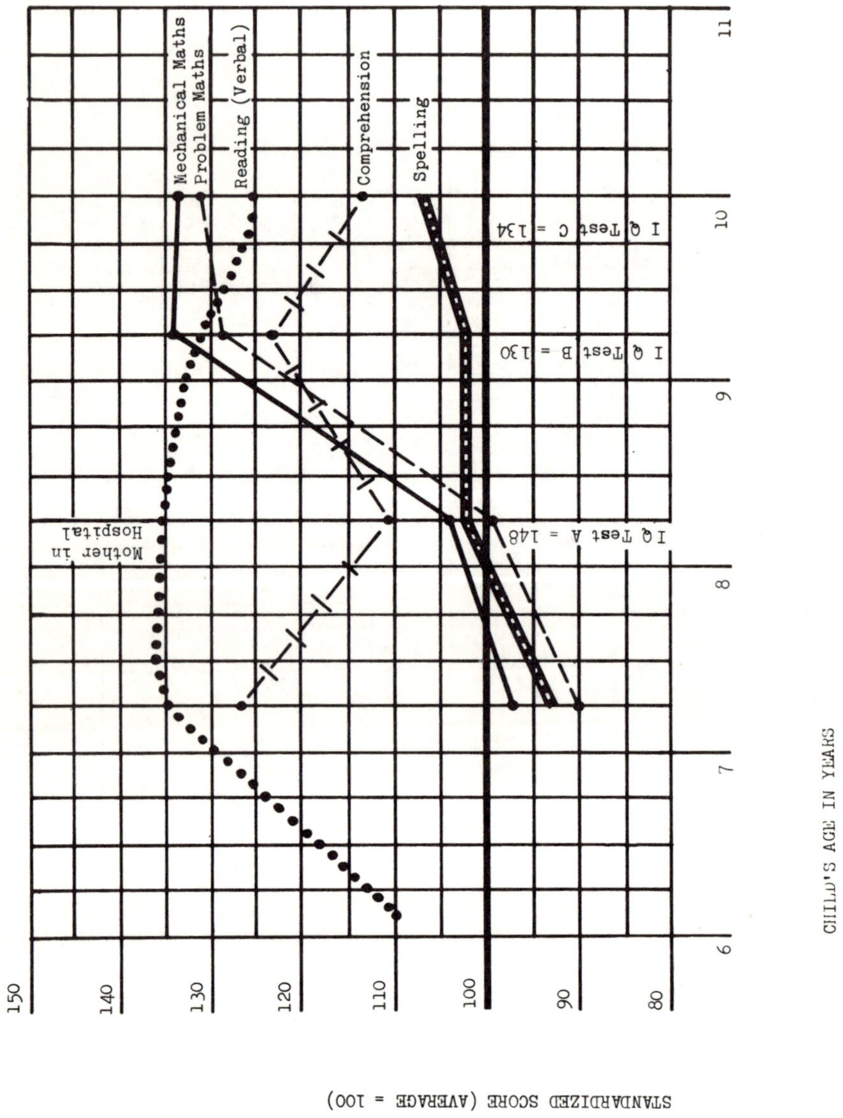

A graph of attainment scores

This graph shows how standardized attainment scores can be employed to provide a visual record of a child's progress in various basic subjects.

The method is both simple and effective and can provide a solid basis upon which an assessment of a child's potential can be made. When an entire class is recorded in this manner, the graphs produced give an outstandingly comprehensive picture of each child's academic ability because each one is easy to interpret visually. This interpretation is made even easier if a different colour is used for each subject recorded on the graph.

General comment

To produce this type of graph entails a considerable amount of work as the standardized tests have to be bought, given to the children, marked, raw scores converted, final score recorded as per the example shown on page 79, and finally the individual graphs have to be constructed. With this amount of work entailed, it might be wiser to maintain this kind of record only when there is a specific reason for so doing.

Recording the academic attainment level of a school

Once standardized tests have been administered to assess the EQ of each child in the class, they can then be recorded on a histogram. If these histograms are completed each year, they will show the progress of each class through the school. The children's initials and chronological age provide a quick cross reference to the more detailed information contained in the record shown on page 81.

As suitable attainment records are not available for the lower classes of the junior school, a record of the verbal reading scores obtained from either the Schonell, or Holborn Verbal Reading test can provide a reasonably reliable indication of the potential of such classes.

General comment

Producing such a record will entail a considerable amount of work and usually its results will only be of interest to the headteacher or members of staff introducing new methods of teaching into the school. It could however be very useful where the population surrounding the school is rapidly changing in character. In many cases the need for additional remedial staff could be securely founded on the information this type of record displays.

Record of the academic level of Fordbury Primary School in May 1970

This record is based upon the individual attainment scores of the children, and each child's educational quotient is shown

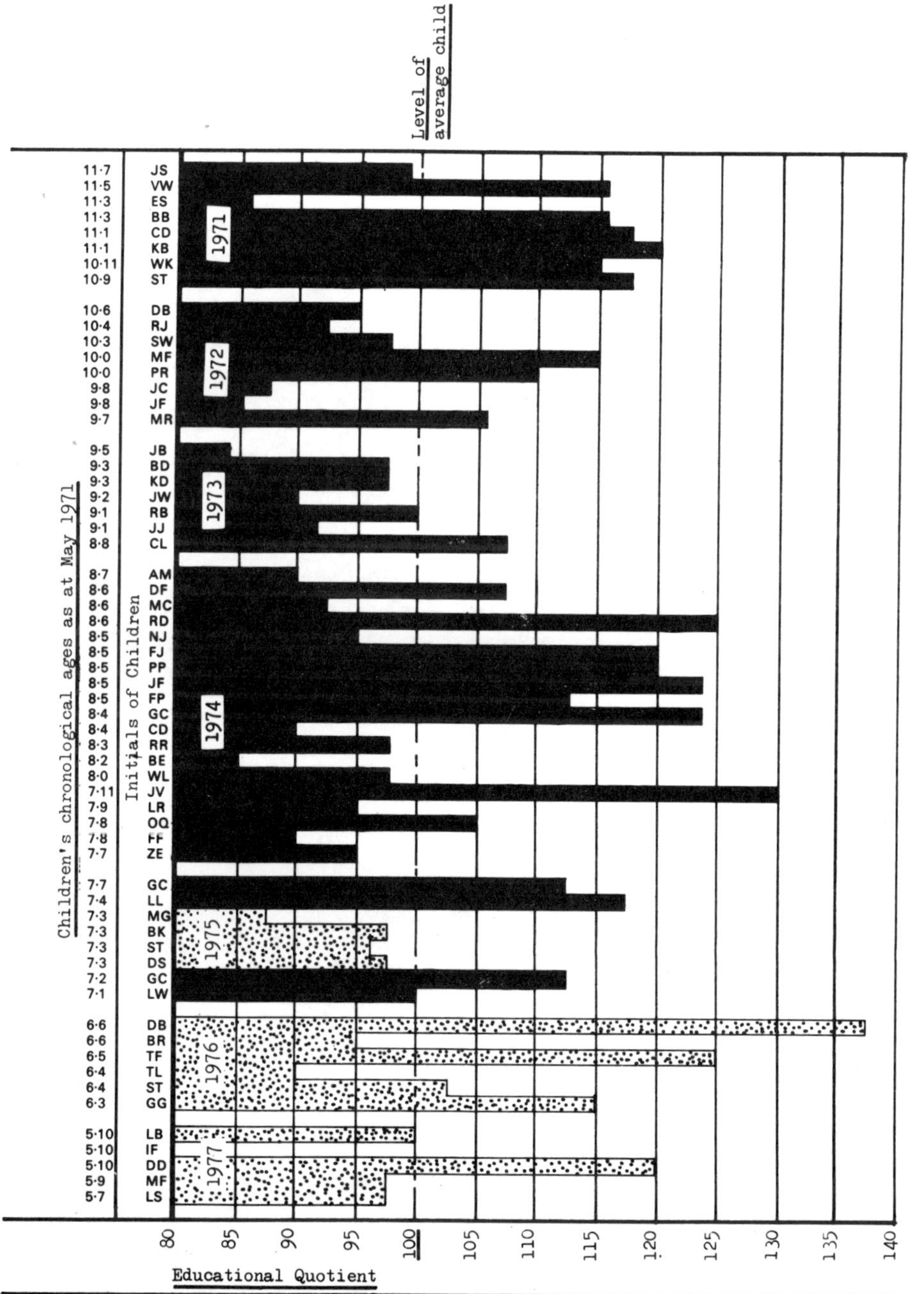

Recording the results of NFER tests

This record illustrates a simple method of recording the scores obtained from NFER tests on a yearly basis.

It is useful where children are not segregated into classes but are grouped according to their need for a particular learning environment, such as the integrated day. Where such a record is produced annually over a period of four years it will be possible to trace a child's academic progress through the school on only four sheets of paper.

Fordbury Primary School : Attainment record for an 'all age group' class

Class Mrs P. Rankin Date of tests 1 May Year 1970

Name	Chron. age	Mechanl. maths		Mathematics progress tests						Primary verbal 1	Primary verbal 2	Primary verbal 3	Non verbal
		A2	A1	A2	A1	B2	B1	C2	C1				
Lebster J.	7.0			119	117					113			
Firk K.	7.1			112	115					110			
Lea M.	7.1			110	104					102			
Datar J.	7.7			107	103					106			
Wood H.	8.0	121	101	115	109								
Packs I.	8.4	143	136	141	138								
Ketch L.	8.4	131	136	128	128								
Williams B.	8.6	125	108	111	113								
Turner F.	8.9	127	116	120	123								
West D.	8.9	137	135	129	130								
Smith Y.	8.9	102	96	98	96								
Tooly D.	9.0	89	93	91	88								
Ward E.	9.2					106	100			105			104
Barts V.	9.3					103	101			100			103
Kirk Y.	9.4					123	113			110			119
Cross E.	9.7					120	117			128			125
Ross B.	9.7					123	129			138			109
Atkins N.	9.9							106	98			105	
Walters F.	9.9							118	103			116	
Peters S.	10.6					79	79			84			
Jones T.	10.7							101	103			100	
Green T.	10.8							102	92			98	

Teacher's comments (with date and initials)

Susan Peters was given easier tests because she had just entered the school and the standard of her work was low. P.R. 6 May 1970.

Recording swimming attainment

This record has been evolved as a result of the continuing growth of interest in teaching swimming in primary schools. In fact the list of swimming awards at the top of the sheet has been compiled as a result of many years experience with the swimming capabilities of primary children. However, the main requirements for the success of this record is that it should be placed where it can be maintained by the children.

Provided the teaching staff do not over emphasize its importance, the record encourages each child to make a real effort to improve upon his past performance. As the ability to swim appears to have no direct relationship with a child's intelligence it is often a source of pride among the less able children who can swim well.

General comment

Some teachers may feel that this kind of record follows too closely the pattern of the old fashioned class lists of weekly attainment and can produce the same evil effects. This can happen in a semi-formal or formal atmosphere but where a truly informal atmosphere has been combined with an integrated method of teaching, the only effect this record seems to produce is group pride in the general level of an age group's swimming ability.

Fordbury Primary School: Swimming record 1970

Name	Half a width	Width	25 yds (30 m)	100 yds (120 m)	$\frac{1}{4}$ mile (400 m)	$\frac{1}{2}$ mile (800 m)	Proficient at diving	ASA Bronze Survival	ASA Silver Survival	STA Junior Swimmer	STA Cadet Swimmer	STA Complete Swimmer	RLS Prelim. Survival	RLS Adv. Survival
10+														
Linda G.	✓	✓	✓	✓	✓	✓	✓	✓	✓	✓	✓			
Neil H.	✓	✓	✓	✓	✓	✓	✓	✓		✓	✓			
Barry J.	✓	✓	✓	✓	✓	✓								
Elinor B.	✓	✓	✓	✓	✓	✓								
Kevin S.	✓	✓	✓	✓	✓	✓	✓	✓		✓	✓			
Peter S.	✓	✓	✓	✓	✓	✓	✓	✓	✓	✓	✓	✓		
Marion L.	✓	✓	✓	✓	✓	✓	✓	✓		✓	✓			
Christine J.	✓	✓	✓	✓	✓	✓	✓	✓		✓	✓			
Terry T.	✓	✓	✓	✓										
9+														
Nicholas J.	✓	✓	✓	✓	✓					✓				
Rosemary H.	✓	✓	✓	✓	✓					✓	✓			
Mickey K.	✓	✓	✓	✓	✓					✓				
Mary H.	✓	✓	✓	✓										
Noreen C.	✓	✓	✓	✓										
Diana S.	✓	✓	✓	✓						✓				
Shane S.	✓	✓	✓	✓										
Mari J.	✓	✓	✓							✓				
Roderick W.	✓	✓	✓	✓						✓				
David A.	✓	✓												
Judith R.	✓	✓	✓											
Graham C.	✓	✓												
Elizabeth M.														
8+														
Simon W.	✓	✓	✓											
Stephen H.	✓													
Geoffrey J.	✓	✓												
Oliver H.	✓	✓	✓	✓										
Karen H.	✓													
Pauline T.	✓	✓												
Diane D.														
Rachel B.	✓	✓												
Karen S.	✓													
Alison C.	✓	✓												
Martin P.	✓													
Michael J.														

A headteacher's report to the school governors

Secrecy is the quickest means of causing misunderstanding between a headteacher and his governors, followed closely by the absence of any record of past events.

A good headteacher's report can dispel both of these problems and provide the headteacher with a legally recognized record of the school's activities as well as a platform from which to launch his own ideas and opinions.

As a record of the school, the report becomes a synopsis of all that takes place and as such can be sent to any officer of the LEA or Department of Education and Science if necessary. Obviously it reflects the official school log book to a certain extent, but the fact that it can be duplicated and posted to individual governors before a meeting makes it a far more useful tool.

The following example of such a report shows how it can be laid out to produce the maximum effect with the minimum of reading.

Numbering the subheadings is important because if the same pattern is followed each time it facilitates immediate reference to a previous report or a specific item of interest. Similarly the reference number 2/69 indicates the number of the report issued and the year in which it was written. The general report at the end must always be brief and can be left out entirely if nothing worthy of comment has occurred.

General comment

Some headteachers may need to use considerable discretion with this type of report but where such conditions exist they usually feed upon half digested facts and rumour. In fact there can be no better use for a record, or report, than if by presenting the facts it can remove this kind of atmosphere from a school.

REPORT 2/69

Headteacher's report on Fordbury Primary School for period 1st February 1969 to 1st July 1969

1 VISITORS

13th February	Miss I. Higgs, Teridge Bury College of Education
20th February	Mr N.W. Karr, A E O
28th March	Mr E. Make, Primary Schools Adviser
4th June	Ten teachers from Bedfordshire L E A
2nd July	Eight students from Teridge Bury College of Education

2 SCHOOL ORGANIZATION

Children on roll	78
Teaching staff	No change
Domestic staff	No change

3 EDUCATIONAL DETAILS

1st, 2nd, 3rd February	25 children and four staff held an Environmental Studies weekend at Hitchin Priory.
4th, 5th February	Mr J. Jones and Mrs S.Smith attended an RI course.
6th February	Bryn Theatre players performed two pl ys for entire school in hall.
13th February	Headmaster lectured to students at Howell College of Education.
1st, 2nd, 22nd, 23rd March	Headmaster ran a four day course on topic work at Cambridge Institute of Education. Has now received an invitation to run a similar course this autumn.
3rd to 5th March	Mrs L.Mann attended RI course.
20th March	Mrs R.Kichen and Mrs B. Dean talked to the entire school on care of teeth.
25th March (half day)	Mrs S.Field attended swimming course.
2nd March	Infants and lower juniors went to London Zoo.
13th to 15th May	Mrs J. Jones attended Offley Course.
2nd June	Eight students from Teridge Bury College of Education stayed the entire day at this school.

4 SCHOOL BUILDINGS

a Extension to school playing field completed except for minor work near playground

b County Architect has completed tentative plans for replacement of buildings

c New electrical work (see previous report 1/69) now completed

d Estimate received for new storage facilities

Future possible commitments

a New large store - estimated cost £170

b Plans for extensions approved by governors

c External painting of school due

d Small swimming pool required

e Large external sandpit needed

5 FURNITURE

We have now completed a seven-year task for re-equipping the school with reasonable furniture and facilities. A television set has been received from county supplies.

6 HEALTH

Dr A. Craw held her termly medical examination.

Mrs S. Drag, automatrician, visited the school April 30th.

7 FILMS

A short coloured film has been made of the children working in school which can be shown to parents etc, as a part of our attempt to involve them in our activities.

8 MUSIC

11th June Mr F. Mark and Mr K. John gave a recital of piano and trombone music to entire school.

8th July Mr and Mrs L. Green gave a recorded recital to children.

9 STUDENT - HALLS PARK COLLEGE OF EDUCATION

Miss G. Vale worked with upper juniors from April 25th to June 6th. She proved to be a very good student.

10 TRANSFER TO SECONDARY SCHOOL

No problems, except that it looks as if it will be increasingly difficult to provide places for highly intelligent children whose parents do not wish them to enter a single sex school.

11 SWIMMING

For the fifth year running all children leaving the school will be able to swim and we seem well set for at least one Dolphin Award.

12 ROAD SAFETY

1st April	H C C Police gave children a talk on road safety.
8th, 9th, 10th, 11th April (Easter Holiday)	Police ran a road safety course in school for children.
21st May	Police presented Cycling Proficiency Awards to 25 children during a road safety evening at which many parents and friends were present.

GENERAL COMMENT

As I have indicated in my reports, the school has been developing a fresh approach to education over a period of years and this has been considerably helped by all members of the staff attending a number of courses as well as paying visits to other schools to observe the general trend of new ideas.

Unfortunately the present buildings are limiting the development of some of our teaching techniques and we all look forward to the facilities which the new building extensions will give us.

Three dimensional record keeping

This illustration has been included in this book simply as a means of showing how children who wish to record three factors at the same time can achieve their goal with a three dimensional histogram.

With this example the vertical blocks representing weight were actually blocks of wood glued on to the histogram so that hours, distance and weight become interrelated.

The various relationships connected with the metric system e.g. 1000 cm^3 = 1 litre of water = 1000 gms—can also be displayed in this way.

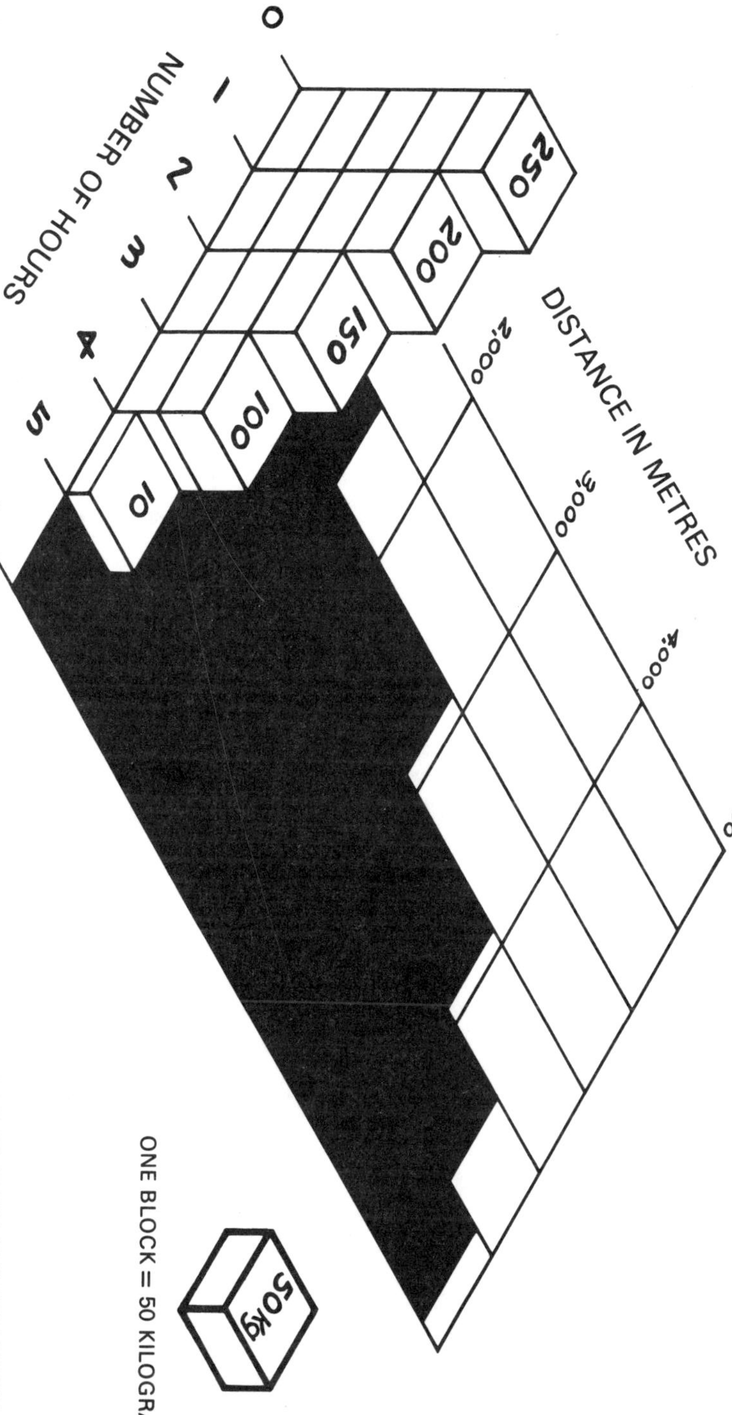

DIAGRAMMATIC VIEW OF CHILD'S THREE DIMENSIONAL RECORD OF A MAN'S ABILITY TO CARRY WEIGHT

Bibliography

Scottish Education Department *Pupils' Progress Records* (HMSO 1969)
L. Keating *The School Report* (K. Mason 1969)
M. Stevens *Observing Children Who Are Severely Subnormal* (E. Arnold 1968)
Pupil Accounting for Local and State Schools Systems (US Department of Health, Education and Welfare 1964)
R. Barn and H. Bernard *Evaluation Techniques for Classroom Teachers* (McGraw 1958)
A. Walker *Pupils' School Records* (Newnes 1955)
W. Glassey and E. Weeks *The Educational Development of Children* (ULP 1950)
W. Stephenson *Testing School Children* (Longmans 1949)
C. Fleming *Cumulative Records* (ULP 1945)
H. Hamley, R. Oliver, H. Field, S. Issacs *The Educational Guidance of the School Child* (Evans 1937)

The books above are listed in the order in which they were published, starting with the most recent.

Index

Numbers in *italics* refer to diagrams

academic attainment 20, 78
  recording of 78, *81*
activity record sheet 72, *73*
assignment cards 63, *64*, *65*
attainment scores *76*, 77

'Bindfast' plastic bars 40

cameras 28
  cine 27
  Kodac Instamatic 28
cassette tape recorders 27
class activities 51, *52*
classwork
  storing 21
colour slides 28
'cross out' records 26-27, *54*, *57*, *61*, *62*, *64-65*, *67-68*, *70-71*
cumulative records 13-14, 28

data cards 27, 42, *43*, *44*, *45*
'date ordered' record books 25
discovery record sheet 72, *73*

educational reports 40, *41*
emotional problems 18

family grouping 13, 60
filmstrips 27

graphs 25-26, *76*, *79*, *89*

headteacher
  report of 18, 20, 84, *85-88*
  role of 18
health record 17
histograms 25-26
  three dimensional 88, *89*

indexed record books 25
informal teaching methods 16
integrated day 13
  child's record of 49, *50*
  teacher's record of 46, *47*

mathematics records 66, *67*, *68*
  in the infant school 60, *61*, *62*
  kept by the child 69, *70*, *71*
  of assignment cards 63, *64*, *65*
multiple choice records 26-27, *54*, *57*, *61*, *62*, *64-65*, *67-68*, *70-71*

NFER tests
  recording the results of 80, 81

personality records 18, 36, *37*
  multiple choice 38, *39*
  pre-school 33, *34*, *35*
photographic records 27

physical development 17
pie diagrams 26, 46, *47*
pre-school profile 33, *34*, *35*
Pupils Progress Records 28

reading
  recording progress 53, *54*, *55*, 56, *57*
  schemes 53, 56
  workshop 58
    record sheet 58, *59*
record keeping
  by children 19, 49, *50*, 69, *70*, *71*, 88, *89*
  problems 13
  reasons for 14-15
  teaching methods 14
  time factor involved 17
  what to avoid 16
  what to do 15-16
  what to record 17-18
remedial staff 78

Scholastic Souvenir Company 27
school
  governors 84
  secretary 19-20
Scottish Education Department 28
social background 18
standardized tests 74
  records of *75*, *76*
storage 19
swimming records 82, *83*

tape recordings 27
Teacher's Record Book 25
Teaching by Topics 19
team teaching 15, 19, 51
topic work 28

video tape 28
visual display 25